Michael
& Amy
Smalley

with *Mike Yorkey*

DON'T DATE NAKED

Tyndale House Publishers, Inc. Wheaton, Illinois

Visit Tyndale's exciting Web site at www.tyndale.com

Don't Date Naked

Published in association with the literary agency of Alive Communications, Inc., 7680 Goddard Street, Suite 200, Colorado Springs, CO 80920.

Designed by Luke Daab

Edited by Lynn Vanderzalm

Some of the names and details in the illustrations used in this book have been changed to protect the privacy of the people in the stories.

Library of Congress Cataloging-in-Publication Data

Smalley, Michael.
   Don't date naked / Michael and Amy Smalley.
      p. cm.
Summary: Uses personal stories, humor, and straight talk to describe all aspects of
dating from a Christian perspective, emphasizing that dating should be good, clean fun.
Includes bibliographical references.
   ISBN 0-8423-5533-2
1. Dating (Social customs)—Religious aspects—Christianity. [1. Dating (Social customs)—Religious aspects—Christianity. 2. Christian life.] I. Smalley, Amy. II. Title.
   HQ801 .S63 2003
   248.8′4—dc21   2003007702

Printed in the United States of America

08 07 06 05 04 03
8   7   6   5   4   3   2   1

CONTENTS

ACKNOWLEDGMENTS

Thanks to Mike Yorkey. What a writer, friend, and encourager. You are the reason the pages in this book came to life. We can never thank you enough for making our dream of helping singles around this country become a reality. You honored our voices and made the book an absolute enjoyment to work on!

Thanks also to Lynn Vanderzalm. When we first heard that Lynn, editor extraordinaire from Tyndale, would be working on our book, we knew we'd reached the big leagues. You are the best! You tore away the layers and molded our sometimes chaotic advice into something of true value for the readers. Thank you for your time and patience.

Finally, thanks to Tyndale House Publishers for allowing us to speak our voice from the mountaintops of publishing. Thank you, Ron Beers, Ken Petersen, and the entire Tyndale staff.

—Michael and Amy Smalley

INTRODUCTION

MICHAEL SAYS

My brother, Greg, is five years older than I am and nearly my opposite in personality type. Throughout high school he was a party animal.

I was a total opposite. I lacked confidence around girls, and I averted my eyes lest my shyness be manifested by an inadvertent glance. I think I had kissed only one girl going into high school.

Greg, who headed for the University of Oklahoma following graduation, returned home that first Christmas feeling like a stud. He must have been pumping iron with the football team because he returned as a buff 160-pounder. He was also in great shape because he was playing a he-man's sport at Oklahoma—rugby.

Greg's love life wasn't too shabby, either. During his freshman year he had two girls on a string: a girl he had met at the dorms in Norman and a winsome young woman back home in Phoenix. *Talk about a dame in every port.*

As soon as he stepped inside the front door for his Christmas break, Greg was all over me. "Hey, are you taking anyone out?"

"No." I was a high school student still getting used to my new school.

"When are you going to start dating somebody?"

"I don't know." I wasn't liking this conversation at all.

"How come? Can't you find anyone good enough for you?"

"Leave me alone, Greg."

"No, I won't. Tell you what. Let's go out on a double date."

"You know that I'm not dating anybody."

"Do you like anyone at school?"

Greg's question caused me to pause. "Well, there's this girl named Stacy. She sits next to me in geometry."

"Then ask her out."

"I'm not asking her out." *I'm shy, doofus!*

"Yes, you are."

"No, I'm not."

"I'm giving you three days to ask her out on a date. If you don't do it, I'll . . ." Greg let the threat hang in the air. I knew my big brother could come up with something embarrassing.

On the third day I worked up enough nerve to approach Stacy in the school hallway.

"Um . . . um . . . Stacy?" I felt so embarrassed, but I knew that if I didn't ask her out, Greg would tell her something terrible about me.

Then Stacy smiled, and I relaxed—but only for a moment. When I remembered what I was there for, my face turned red, and I could feel sweat forming above my lip. "Stacy, I was wondering . . . you probably don't want to do this, and it would be okay if you said no, and I'm sure it won't be any fun, but my brother's back home from college, and he's making me ask somebody out, so I thought I might ask you. What do you think? Do you want to do something on Saturday night?"

Without any hesitation Stacy replied, "Yeah, that sounds like it would be fun."

Oh, no!

Instead of feeling really happy that I had nabbed a date, I felt totally stressed out. I would be going out on a double date with a modern-day Romeo!

A few days later we picked up our dates and drove to a nice steak house not far from our home. I sat in the back with Stacy, where we listened to Greg keep up a steady patter. I didn't say a word because I didn't *want* to talk: I was surrounded by people who were cooler and much better looking than I was, so I thought it would be better if I didn't call attention to myself by saying something stupid.

After we were seated at the restaurant, the hostess handed us our menus. We placed our orders and were directed to a generous salad bar. I followed Stacy through the line, but I still hadn't uttered two words. After piling my plate high with Caesar salad, I noticed some watermelon. I had to have some of that. I stabbed at a triangular piece with a fork, and when I lifted it up, I noticed that another wedge of watermelon was stuck to it. Stacy turned toward me as I tried to flick off the hanging piece of watermelon. I jerked my wrist to fling the fruit back onto the tray, but that second wedge of watermelon flew through the air and smacked Stacy in the forehead. For what seemed like an eternity, the fruit stuck to her forehead like a cold compress.

To my horror, the watermelon wedge slowly slid down the bridge of her cute nose before dropping to the floor.

"Stacy! I'm so sorry—"

"Michael, don't worry about it," she said, as she dabbed herself with a napkin. "I'm going to be okay." With that, Stacy kicked the offending piece of sticky fruit under the buffet table. "Well, I never did like watermelon in my salad anyway," she said.

That sealed the deal for me. Stacy was not only cool but also a bit crazy like me. I gradually came out of my shell, and we dated for several years. We had a solid, great relationship.

Sitting on a Park Bench

Dating, to play off a phrase uttered by Forrest Gump, is like a box of chocolates: You never know what you're going to get. In a similar way, you never know if a date will be a fun experience or something that makes you gag.

I grew up in a home where dating was not only part of growing up but also an activity encouraged by my mom and dad. I dated steadily from my freshman year of high school until I married at age twenty-one. My parents never made me feel embarrassed about liking girls or wanting to go out with them.

"Wow! You're interested in this new girl!" my dad would exclaim from the dinner table. "That's cool, Michael. Let's have her over for a swim and barbecue thing, or maybe we can take her out for some Mexican food with us. We'd love to meet her."

That's how my parents were. They *loved* meeting the girls I took out and hearing how my dates turned out afterward. They often said things such as, "I really like her," or "She seems like a nice girl."

We Still Love Dating

My wife, Amy, and I are all for dating, and in this book we'll make the case for going out. We believe that dating will provide you with awesome life experiences, teach you how to talk and interact with the opposite sex, and help you mature into someone who will be ready to get married at the appropriate time.

It's amazing what you learn about another person when you date, although many people do not reveal their inadequacies or their past when they're dating. That's a natural human reaction since none of us seeks rejection from the other sex. It's called putting your best foot forward.

Nevertheless, we must acknowledge that dating has pitfalls, which we will also address. Hey, we know how painful dating can be: I can still remember getting dumped by a girl because she preferred to go out with the high school quarterback—and he was a second-stringer at that! As for Amy, she dated a young man for four years, and they even got engaged before she broke it off. Now that *hurt*.

Contrary to what some other voices say, those experiences don't dampen our enthusiasm for dating—they just make us more aware of who we are and where God is leading us in our lives. To paraphrase something Tennyson once said, "It's better to have dated and lost than never to have dated at all."

Behind the Title

What do you think of our provocative book title—*Don't Date Naked*? I have to credit Jason Brawner, my best friend since my grammar school days, for coming up with it. *Don't Date Naked* is not meant to be taken literally, because never in our wildest dreams would we recommend that a couple date au naturel. The title is drawn from Ephesians 6, where the apostle Paul encourages us to put on the full armor of God so that we will be prepared to stand firm in the spiritual battles we face.

If you need to be reminded about the words in the Ephesians passage, here it is. Read it through with an eye toward the dating relationship.

> Be strong with the Lord's mighty power. Put on all of God's armor so that you will be able to stand firm against all strategies and tricks of the Devil. For we are not fighting against people made of flesh and blood, but against the evil rulers and authorities of the unseen world, against those mighty powers of darkness who rule this world, and against wicked spirits in the heavenly realms.
>
> Use every piece of God's armor to resist the enemy in the time of evil, so that after the battle you will still be standing firm. Stand your ground, putting on the sturdy belt of truth and the body armor of God's righteousness. For shoes, put on the peace that comes from the Good News, so that you will be fully prepared. In every battle you will need faith as your shield to stop the fiery arrows aimed at you by Satan. Put on salvation as your helmet, and take the sword of the Spirit, which is the word of God. Pray at all times and on every occasion in the power of the

Holy Spirit. Stay alert and be persistent in your prayers for all Christians everywhere.

Just as you wouldn't fight naked without the full armor of God, you don't want to date naked without God's protection. If you will allow us some poetic license, we'd like to paraphrase the Ephesians 6 passage for the dating relationship:

> Be strong with the Lord's mighty power. Don't date naked. Clothe yourself with all of the protection God has provided so that you will be able to stand firm against all strategies and tricks of the Devil. For when you date, you will face temptations and challenges that are beyond your ability to fight alone. You will need God's grace, love, wisdom, and power. You will need help from friends who are committed to your good. You will need a special wardrobe for the challenge.
>
> So get dressed. Put on all of the clothing God has provided so that you will stand firm. Stand your ground, putting on the robe of prayer, which will cover you, submitting yourself and your future to God's plan. Next put on the sturdy belt of accountability, which will hold you to your goals. For shoes, put on honor so that you will be able to walk confidently, giving full respect to the people you date. In every dating situation you will need a commitment to purity as your shield to stop the fiery arrows of temptation aimed at you by Satan.
>
> Pray at all times and on every occasion in the power of the Holy Spirit. Stay alert, and be persistent in your prayers.

There you have it—the wardrobe for a successful dating relationship:

- Robe of prayer
- Belt of accountability
- Shoes of honor
- Shield of purity

Throughout this book we'll talk more about how to dress for success in dating.

AMY SAYS

Michael and I understand that dating is controversial in some Christian circles. In recent years, a few authors have made the case for not dating at all—or at least not until the week before you get married. (We're exaggerating, of course, but we'll have more to say in the next chapter about those who say we should kiss dating goodbye.)

The focus in *Don't Date Naked* is to get you to think about why you date, who you should date, when you should date, and why you need to be thinking about where the dating relationship is going. We will do that through sharing some of our stories with you, warning you to avoid some mistakes we made, fielding some questions people have asked us, and at times, having some straight talks about tough issues. At the end of each chapter we've included some "Dear Mike & Amy" letters, specific questions dating people have asked us. You might even find your own story in one of the letters.

Every year in the conferences and seminars we lead, we meet thousands of people who are dating, and we hear some sad stories about poor decisions people have made—decisions that have serious long-term consequences. We want to help you avoid making those same bad choices. We promise to be honest with you, giving straight answers and advice. At times you will feel that we are in your face. That's okay, though. Sometimes that's what it takes.

Reading *Don't Date Naked* will help you:

- know what a godly dating life looks like;
- list personality qualities you want in the people you date;
- honor the person you're dating;

- stay pure by setting healthy physical and emotional limits;
- end a relationship when it's not right;
- think long term;
- dress for success in dating.

In the quest to find that someone special, you need to be thinking intentionally about the qualities that you would want to see in a potential spouse. If guys put as much thought into what type of person they would want to date and eventually marry as they put into researching their next set of wheels, there would be far fewer busted relationships and subsequent divorces. And if young women adopted a more calm and collected, eyes-wide-open approach, they wouldn't fall for the first hunk on the make.

Your late teens and early twenties are the time of your life for you to think about dating intentionally. Decisions about the people you will date could have lifelong implications, so you need to put more thought into this than the next CD player you're going to buy.

The fact that you're holding this book in your hands tells us you're serious about dating. Well, maybe *serious* isn't the right word since you're dating to have some fun and meet some interesting people. Or maybe it *is* the right word because you think you may have found the person you will marry. Wherever you are on the dating front, we're glad you're joining us.

Just don't date naked.

1
let's hear it for dating

They are the hottest forms of "reality TV" out there—the dating shows like *Blind Date*, *ElimiDATE*, *Change of Heart*, *Taildaters*, *The 5th Wheel*, *Shipmates*, and *Dismissed*. When you stop and think about it, what can be more real than watching the sparks fly between a virile pair sexually attracted to each other?

These are not your parents' dating shows, however, like the relatively tame *The Dating Game*, a ripe-for-parody effort that looked as if it was filmed on a cheesy set designed by a hippie coming down off a bad psychedelic trip. No, this rash of new half-hour shows is a whole new genre, filled with dirty talk and lots of sex.

MICHAEL SAYS

I've checked out most of them, but when you've seen one, you've seen them all. The premise usually goes like this: a buff guy, confident and sure of himself to the point of arrogance, is on the hunt. He will be introduced to a motley and well-built foursome of vixens dripping with attitude, and he must choose one to make the Perfect Match. At least, that's what the producers would have us believe happens in this make-believe world where dudes can have anything they want.

Everyone has roles to play. Guys are playboys, and girls are playthings. And they usually end up in a Jacuzzi, where tops and bottoms are flung off, and the sudsy talk revolves around sex. Trashy challenges are given: once on *Elimi-DATE*, the guy made the gals kiss each other if they wanted to reach the next level, but most of the time, the guy chooses the girl who lifts her shirt or performs a suggestive lap dance. These new dating shows are all about voyeurism and spying on the antics of sex-soaked guys and girls searching for love and acceptance in all the wrong places.

Some role models. Unfortunately, too many young people are influenced by this "reality," convinced that these episodes reflect what dating is all about. That's a shame because these "reality dating" programs give a very unreal and unhealthy picture of dating.

Amy and I believe that dating can be clean, wholesome fun, especially when it's done with an attitude of honor. Dating teaches valuable lessons as well: social skills such as manners, the art of conversation, and respect for self-imposed and mutually agreed-on limits for physical expression. And finally, dating almost certainly allows the opportunity for you to get to know the person who could potentially become your husband or wife.

Not everyone agrees with us, however. In recent years there has been a move to embrace a philosophy of "no dating"—at least until you are spiritually mature and financially able to get married. These dating models, known in Christian circles as betrothal and courtship, have become more mainstream in the last decade. Amy will give us a closer look at what they are all about.

AMY SAYS

I have to admit that I hadn't heard of the word *betrothal* until just a few years ago, but what it means is that a couple must wait for God to impress on the guy's heart that a certain young woman—let's call her Missy—is the person he ought to marry. Once God makes that impression on the guy's heart, he is to pray about it. Once he feels that the impression has been confirmed by God, he then approaches the young woman and tells her that God impressed on his heart that they should marry.

Notice that I used a form of the word *impressed* four times in the previous paragraph, but those who buy into betrothal say that word a lot. Michael and I think the concept is flawed, and it's not because we don't think God can speak directly to people today. One of the problems is that betrothal is ripe for abuse. What is a young woman supposed to make of a young suitor who drops into her life and informs her that God told him that they should marry? Sometimes this happens even though the two people have never gone out on an official date. It seems to us that this is taking advantage of her emotions and vulnerability regarding *the* biggest decision she will ever make: *Whom should I marry?*

I've always wondered how I would have felt if some guy had knocked on my door and said that God told him we should get married. Michael and I don't see betrothal or arranged marriages working in our Western culture because individual freedom and choice are two of the bedrock values of our society. Betrothal and arranged marriages just don't work here, just as our dating practices wouldn't work in many other countries. When I was a student at Wheaton College Graduate School, I once had a class with a young man from India. He told me that his parents had arranged his marriage and that he and his wife were introduced to each other a month before they were married. When I expressed my surprise, he replied that he and his wife were raised in India's caste system, and that is how his culture did things.

"How long have you been married?" I asked.

"About ten years," replied my friend. "And we are happy."

I believed him, but I can hardly imagine my parents "arranging" my marriage, although there was a family joke growing up that I would marry Shannon Dobyns. (Don't laugh. Shannon is a boy's name.) The Dobyns family and our family were very tight, and they had a daughter named Samantha, who became my very best friend.

In high school, Samantha and I went out on double dates together. Whenever I dropped by the Dobyns's home to go out on Saturday night, Shannon, who was a few years older, would tease me by saying, "Aren't you going to wait for me?"

"Yeah, and then we could be sisters!" Samantha would exclaim.

No offense to Shannon since he's a cool guy, but I'm sure glad that no parental matchmaking ever happened or that Shannon did not feel "impressed" by God that we should get hitched.

No, I was raised by normal parents who allowed me to double-date as a freshman and "car date" a year later. Back then, betrothal was not on the radar screen for Christian families, and neither was the concept of courtship.

What is meant by *courtship?* In one of the popular models of courtship, a guy and a girl don't date until they are spiritually and financially ready to get married—and when they do date, it's under heavy parental authority. For younger people, this, in effect, means no dating in high school and the first few years of college—and possibly not until you're established in some sort of a career track.

Here's how courtship works in this model: If you're a guy and you've had your eye on Missy for quite some time—and are spiritually and financially prepared to marry if you fall in love with her—then you approach her father (or her mother if the father is out of the picture) and announce your intentions. Both men pray about it, and if the father agrees that you are spiritually and financially ready for marriage, you are allowed to date the young woman. Usually the dating is done in the context of family activities, like going to church or joining the family on a picnic at the lake, something like that. As for casual one-on-one dates with a movie followed by a Starbucks latté, forget about it.

This courtship model was the centerpiece of Joshua Harris's successful book *I Kissed Dating Goodbye*, an auto-biographical account that urged young people to forego the dating scene entirely, just as he did. Published in the mid-1990s, *I Kissed Dating Goodbye*'s influence has penetrated the Christian culture. We're constantly running into young people who say they've read it—or that their parents are insisting that they adhere to their wishes by following the courtship model.

We believe that courtship and betrothal are often based on parental fear. The No Dating sign gets hung across the front door because the parents fear that their child will meet the wrong person, suffer emotional trauma when the relationship ends, or become sexually involved. We don't deny that those are valid concerns for parents, especially for young teens starting to navigate the high school years. But once you get into college and your early twenties, you need to learn to make your *own* decisions.

Sure, some of those decisions will result in mistakes and regret, possibly even some lifelong pain. But our hope is that since you're reading this book, you're willing to listen to our advice so that when it comes time to make choices, you will make decisions that honor God, your dating partner, and yourself.

MICHAEL
SAYS

I remember the first time I picked up a copy of Josh's book, eager to find out if he really meant that we should kiss dating goodbye. Yes, he meant it. Josh wrote that it didn't make sense training for a long-term relationship—marriage—with a series of short-term dating relationships. He said it would be like practicing how to break up and that each time you experienced an agonizing breakup, you lost a part of your heart that could never be reclaimed.

That's a good speech, but Amy and I have a different perspective. Dating, like nearly everything else in life, has the capacity for good and evil. We, along with millions of others, have had extremely positive experiences in our dating relationships. We also checked into Heartbreak Hotel a few times. Does that mean that dating was bad? No.

Having said that, we agree with Joshua Harris about dating in more ways than you would think, but Amy and I think that it's okay to date *some* and go on group dates in your young adult years. The difference is that we think you should wait to date *seriously* until you are at an age at which you could marry.

The reason that dating is not all cut-and-dried is because dating is a fairly recent social phenomenon. Before the early part of the twentieth century, guys and girls didn't always date—it wasn't allowed by shotgun-toting fathers who put the fear of God into men wishing to "court" their daughters.

We are exaggerating, of course, but try to imagine what rural and city life were like in America before the rise of the Industrial Age. In a more rural America, education usually ended by the time a young man or woman reached the age of fourteen. If you were a guy, it was off to the fields, where hard labor awaited you.

From sunup to sundown, you stared at the south end of a horse traveling north, and then you shared a bed with a pair of unbathed younger brothers. If you were a young woman, you milled flour and cooked and cleaned, and cared for the younger siblings. Who could blame someone for having the itch to get married and get out of the house?

Those who struck out on their own before marrying were ostracized. The word *bachelor* was pejorative in those days; to be single while of "marrying age" was a sign of laziness—you either couldn't attract someone to marry or you lacked the ability to support a wife and family. Authorities harassed bachelors by running them out of town on a rail.

The courting scene began changing in a hurry during the 1920s—the Roaring Twenties. As families moved to the cities and something called "suburbs" popped up like marigolds following a spring shower, young people were expected to finish high school. Many more young people moved on to college. The ties to home and hearth were loosened, and the rise of cheap transportation (the Model T Ford) and cheap entertainment (the movies) gave young people the mobility and the opportunity to partici-pate in informal, unchaperoned male-female activities without any sort of commitment.

AMY SAYS

For the first time in the history of man-kind, the concept of modern dating emerged. So you see, dating *is* a fairly recent development—and it didn't take long for a new set of rituals to develop. Young men could seek whoever made their hearts quicken without nosy parents trying to "arrange" a match. Young women held the balance of power, however: they could pick and choose the person they wanted to date, although they no longer had a doting father screening out the bad apples. Without parental supervision, guys became more adept at pushing the physical boundaries, and couples experienced premarital sex in unprecedented numbers. As the number of out-of-wedlock pregnancies climbed, the phrase "shot-gun marriage" became part of the lexicon.

Dating continued to evolve over the next fifty years, and when your parents came of age in the rock 'n' roll six-ties and disco seventies, the doors were blown off. This became known as the era of "free love." With fewer social constraints holding young couples back, it was common for a guy to meet a girl at a Vietnam peace demonstration, head back to her apartment, roll around in the sack, and then ask, "What did you say your name was?"

How ironic when she answered, "Chastity."

"Free love" eventually gave way to the phenomenon of living together, which is where we are today. Between 1960 and 1997, the number of cohabiting couples went from fewer than 500,000 to 4 million—an eye-popping 800 percent increase, according to the U.S. Census Bureau.[1] These days, more than 50 percent of first marriages are preceded by cohabitation, according to University of Wisconsin researchers Larry Bumpass and Hsien-Hen Lu.[2]

Michael and I work with young people at our church and speak to thousands of young people all over the country. It's our goal to reverse the trend of living together and to instill godly ideals about what dating relationships should look like. When done right, dating can play a significant role in who you become and whom you eventually marry, which is why we feel so passionate about the issue.

MICHAEL SAYS Dating is fun, and during your late teens and into your twenties, it *should* be fun. I remember the time when I arrived on the campus of Baylor University as a freshman, ready to make friends and experience the college scene after attending a small K–12 Christian school in Phoenix. I wasn't looking to sow any wild oats, but I was ready for something different.

During the fall quarter, the school held a "Howdy

Dance"—a mixer where the girls ask the boys out. When a popular girl asked me to be her date, I thought, *Wow, that's pretty cool.* I knew we wouldn't be marrying; we were just going out to have some fun.

She and I agreed to go with a group to the Elite Café, the most popular eating establishment at Baylor, before the big dance. The Elite Café was one of those diner-type restaurants that serves comfort foods like meatloaf, baby-back ribs, country-fried steak, mashed potatoes, and soft dinner rolls by the basketful.

As raucous college kids often do, we guys decided to play a little game. We played Rock, Scissors, Paper to see who would be the first victim. Whoever lost had to stuff an entire basket of dinner rolls in his mouth. Each basket contained four or five rolls, each the size of a baseball.

Top ten *worst* Christian pick-up lines for guys

10. That's a nice Bible you have. What translation is it?

9. May I show you my promise ring?

8. Jesus said when you do something for the least of these, you do it for him. How about going out to dinner with me?

7. Would you like to be my accountability partner?

6. Have you been going to this church a long time?

5. Would it be a sin if you stole my heart?

4. Could I show you my video collection of Billy Graham Crusades?

3. What's the name of your Compassion child?

2. Have you seen my "What Would Jesus Do" bracelet?

1. Excuse me, but I think one of your ribs belongs to me.

Unfortunately I lost, so I began stuffing the rolls into my mouth, just like Paul Newman eating hard-boiled eggs in *Cool Hand Luke*. I punched two or three rolls down the hatch, chewed, and then tried to swallow the biggest clump of dough ever, but it stuck in my throat. I started doing some serious choking. Now, of course, I was humiliated.

My friend Brodie screamed out, "Look, Smalley's choking!" Everyone panicked, and then Brodie began pounding my back. I remember thinking that I would die and that it was a horrible way to go. Out of sheer desperation, I took a big swallow and shoved the gigantic dough ball down my gullet, tearing up my throat in the process. I survived, but I couldn't talk for the rest of the night. Needless to say, I embarrassed myself in front of the young woman who had invited me to the dance.

I didn't go out with that young woman again, but I don't think I left a piece of my heart with her. Our date was good, clean fun, and that's what dating should be all about.

Amy and I have come up with six positive reasons why we think you should date:

1. *Dating should be a source of enjoyment and recreation.* Whatever you enjoy doing—going to movies, taking in a concert, going for a walk, exploring museums, participating in sporting events—do it with your date. As you are involved together in things you both enjoy, you will get to know each other better and become more comfortable with each other.

2. Dating is a big part of the socialization process. You gain social confidence when you learn manners, how to be considerate of others, and how to carry on a conversation with a member of the opposite sex. Said in another way, dating teaches guys how to open car doors and quit chewing gum in public, and it allows girls to dress nicely and receive special treatment.

3. Dating helps personality development and learning of gender roles. Personal identity is developed through relationships with other people. Young men and women need to discover the kinds of roles they find fulfilling in a close relationship. This can be accomplished through interaction with the opposite sex.

4. Dating involves learning about intimacy and serves as an opportunity to establish a unique, meaningful relationship with a person of the opposite sex. God created us with a need for relationships. Think about it. When God created the world and assessed his work, he announced that everything was good except for one thing: it was not good for Adam to be alone. God wants us to have deep and meaningful relationships, and marriage, of course, is the deepest relationship two people can have. Every friendship is an opportunity to develop a mature relationship with another person, and when that friendship involves someone of the opposite sex, you can learn about love and honor, sacrifice and tenderness.

5. *Dating helps you find that special person God has planned for you.* Yes, God knows who your future spouse will be, but you are still traveling on a journey in which you meet and form relationships with those of the opposite sex. Dating helps us narrow the field of eligible partners and gives us confidence that we are making the right choice.

6. *Dating can help prepare you for marriage.* We know that Joshua Harris and others may not agree with us here, but we are convinced that dating helps couples acquire the knowledge and skills for a successful marriage. For example, dating helps develop a better understanding of each other's attitudes and behaviors, understand how to get along, and practice discussing and solving relational problems.

Got the basics down? Good, because in our next chapter, we're going to talk about preparing a list of qualities that you would want to see in the person you would date seriously.

Dear Mike & Amy,

Two of my college friends—one a guy and the other a girl—are in courtship relationships (but not with each other). They are pressuring me not to date, trying to convince me that their way is somehow more biblical. They make me feel that I'm less of a Christian if I date in "normal" ways. I've prayed about this, and I do not hear God telling me to stop dating. What should I do, and how do I handle their pressure?

—Confused

DEAR CONFUSED,

PEER PRESSURE IS HARD TO FIGHT, ESPECIALLY IF YOU RESPECT THE OPINIONS OF THOSE WHO ARE PRESSURING YOU. PLEASE DON'T BUY INTO THE IDEA THAT ONE FORM OF DATING IS "MORE BIBLICAL" THAN THE REST. THE SCRIPTURES GIVE US GUIDING PRINCIPLES FOR RELATIONSHIPS—SUCH AS HONOR, PURITY, UNCONDITIONAL LOVE, AND GRACE. BUT THE BIBLE DOES NOT DICTATE *HOW* WE ARE TO FIND THE PERSON WE WILL MARRY, WHETHER THAT BE THROUGH DATING, THROUGH HAVING PARENTS ARRANGE MARRIAGES, OR THROUGH THE MODEL OF COURTSHIP.

HAVING SAID THAT, IF YOU SENSE THAT DATING IS FOR YOU, WE ENCOURAGE YOU TO GET INVOLVED IN HEALTHY DATING RELATIONSHIPS AS A WAY OF FINDING THE PERSON GOD HAS CHOSEN FOR YOU. CONTINUE PRAYING WITH AN EXPECTANT HEART THAT GOD WILL ANSWER YOUR QUESTIONS. JUST BE CAUTIOUS NOT TO ALLOW FEAR TO RULE YOUR EMOTIONS. REMEMBER THAT GOD DIDN'T GIVE US A SPIRIT OF FEAR (SEE 2 TIMOTHY 1:7).

FEAR—EITHER OF YOUR FRIENDS' DISAPPROVAL OR OF MAKING MISTAKES—DOESN'T HAVE TO DRIVE YOU AWAY FROM DATING. EVEN IF YOU'VE MADE MISTAKES IN THE PAST, YOU AREN'T DESTINED TO MAKE THEM AGAIN. IF YOU NEED TO TAKE A BREAK FROM DATING FOR A WHILE, GO AHEAD AND DO THAT. BUT THAT DOESN'T MEAN YOU NEED TO TAKE A BREAK FROM GOD'S DIRECTION IN THAT AREA OF YOUR LIFE. SEARCH FOR GOD'S BEST FOR YOU, NOT FOR ACCEPTANCE FROM YOUR FRIENDS.

—Mike & Amy

Dear Mike & Amy,

I'm a twenty-year-old guy who wants to date, but I'm clueless about how to start. Some of my female friends think I'm not interested in dating, but that's not true. I like many of them, and some of them might even be good wives someday, but I'm scared to start dating because I'm afraid I'll be clumsy at it. Can you help me?

—Clueless

Dear Clueless,

YOU'RE PROBABLY NOT AS CLUMSY AS YOU THINK YOU ARE. WE ALL WERE NERVOUS WHEN WE FIRST STARTED DATING. IT SOUNDS AS IF YOU HAVE SOME GOOD FEMALE FRIENDS, THOUGH. WOULD YOU CONSIDER ASKING THEM OUT? MAYBE YOU COULD BROACH THE SUBJECT WITH ONE OF THEM; SAY SOMETHING LIKE, "WE'VE BEEN FRIENDS FOR A LONG TIME, AND WE LIKE A LOT OF THE SAME THINGS. WOULD YOU CONSIDER GOING OUT WITH ME OCCASIONALLY?" IF SHE SAYS NO, DON'T FALL APART AND FEEL AS IF YOU ARE SOME SORT OF REJECT. YOU'RE NOT.

MAYBE SOME OF YOUR GOOD FEMALE FRIENDS COULD HELP YOU FIND SOMEONE TO DATE. ASK THEM FOR SUGGESTIONS. YOU MIGHT BE SURPRISED BY THEIR ANSWERS, BUT TAKE THEM TO HEART. YOUR FRIENDS MAY KNOW YOU BETTER THAN YOU KNOW YOURSELF.

OR, IF YOU HAVE FRIENDS WHO ARE DATING, ASK THEM FOR IDEAS. MAYBE YOU COULD EVEN DOUBLE-DATE. THEN TAKE IT A STEP FURTHER, AND ASK YOUR FRIENDS—GUYS AND GIRLS—TO COACH YOU THE DAY AFTER ON A FEW THINGS THEY MAY HAVE DONE DIFFERENTLY AND THE THINGS THEY REALLY LIKED. GIRLS LOVE TO HELP AND WILL EAT THIS UP! AND THIS IS A GOOD WAY TO GET CLOSE TO YOUR COACH TOO!

—Mike & Amy

don't date naked

What if I don't know whether or not I want to get married? Can I still date for the sake of companionship? Or since dating is supposed to lead to marriage, should I not date at all?

—Unsure about dating

Dear Unsure,

WE ARE DESIGNED TO BE IN RELATIONSHIPS WITH GOD, SELF, AND OTHERS. WHO THOSE OTHERS ARE DEPENDS ON YOU.

YOU'RE NOT ALONE IN WONDERING WHETHER YOU WANT TO GET MARRIED. WE KNOW SEVERAL PEOPLE, FOR EXAMPLE, WHO ARE WARY OF MARRIAGE BECAUSE THEIR OWN PARENTS' MARRIAGES DIDN'T WORK OUT, AND THEY ARE SCARED OF MAKING THE SAME MISTAKES. THAT FEAR MAY NOT FACTOR INTO YOUR SITUATION, BUT YOU MAY HAVE OTHER FEARS THAT MAY LEAD YOU TO WONDER ABOUT WHETHER MARRIAGE IS FOR YOU.

WE ENCOURAGE YOU NOT TO LET FEAR KEEP YOU FROM DATING. CONTINUE DATING, BUT ALSO CONTINUE PRAYING ABOUT IT.

YOU ARE WISE TO QUESTION WHETHER IT'S ALL RIGHT TO DATE FOR COMPANIONSHIP. SINCE COMPANIONSHIP AND FRIENDSHIP ARE NEEDS WE ALL HAVE, AND SINCE THEY ARE NEEDS THAT HUSBANDS AND WIVES HAVE TOO, DEEP FRIENDSHIPS ARE A HEALTHY FOUNDATION FOR A DATING RELATIONSHIP.

BUT IF YOU ARE LOOKING JUST FOR FRIENDSHIP, BE CAREFUL NOT TO LEAD YOUR DATING PARTNER ON. BE UP FRONT WITH THE COMPANIONS YOU HAVE. GO DUTCH. DON'T FLIRT, AND DON'T GET PHYSICALLY AFFECTIONATE.

ASK GOD WHAT HE THINKS IS BEST FOR YOU AT THIS TIME AND IN THE FUTURE. BE WILLING TO HEAR YOU ARE TOO SELF-FOCUSED TO GIVE YOURSELF TO A RELATIONSHIP RIGHT NOW. ALLOW GOD TO CHANGE YOUR HEART IF HE WANTS.

—Mike & Amy

2

making a list
and checking it twice

We assume that you are either currently dating or want to be dating. If you are currently dating, what drew you to the other person? What four qualities pop into your head right now?

We asked a few people those same questions and got various answers:

- "He's in my Western civilization class. He seems pretty smart. Hmm . . . he's funny, and . . . well . . . he's cute."

- "Let's see, she's so easy to talk to. She likes football. She plays a mean saxophone. And she has the greatest eyes. They make me melt."

- "He seems to have a lot of money, so he can take me fun places. He has traveled a lot with his family and knows people all over the world. He knows where he's going in life, and I think I'd like to go there with him."

- "She's so comfortable to be with; I can talk with her about anything when we're at Starbucks. She likes so many of the same things I do—jazz, hiking, John Grisham novels. She's fun to be around."

If you want to be dating, what will you be looking for in a dating partner? Good looks? Personal wealth? Intelligence? A good sense of humor? Take some time to write a mental list of four things that you'd like to see in someone you'd date.

One of the reasons we think dating is such a good idea is that it gives two people the opportunity to get to know each other better. Plus, it gives people a chance to find that "perfect person" who will become a lifelong marriage partner.

But how will you know if you've met Mr. Right or Ms. Right if you don't know what you're looking for?

We recommend—and we cannot stress this enough—that before you get into a serious dating relationship, you should have a list of qualities that you would want to see in the person you're spending time with—and might eventually want to marry. We call this the Qualities List, and it revolves around the qualities that would be important to you.

AMY
SAYS

This is something I did in a haphazard way when I was a young teenager. It was a great idea, and I'm glad I did it. The only problem was that for a long time I didn't take the list seriously. But when I finally did, it prevented me from making a huge mistake—marrying the wrong person!

My story begins the summer before my junior year of high school when I began dating a guy who had a friend named Jeff, a college freshman at the time. I must have caught Jeff's eye because he told other friends, "I'm going to make that girl fall in love with me." Eighteen months later I wasn't dating Jeff's friend anymore. Jeff was home during Christmas break from the University of Texas at Austin, where he was in his sophomore year. I was in the middle of my senior year at Conroe High, near Houston.

One of Jeff's friends was throwing a party between Christmas and New Year's. All my friends were going, and it sounded like a fun thing to do. Jeff introduced himself, and we must have talked and hung out for a long time because I arrived home late. Mom grounded me for missing curfew.

"Forget about doing anything on New Year's," she said. I was extremely disappointed because Jeff had invited me to see him at this New Year's Eve party. I hatched a plan. I told my older sister, Judy, that I would help her bus tables at the restaurant she worked at since she needed extra help on the biggest party night of the year. Since she lived in an apartment a few miles from our house, I told my parents I would crash at Judy's place after work was done.

Instead of going home after midnight, however, I slunk over to Jeff's party. (I know, not a very honest thing to do.) I thought he was so cool, and to a high school senior, he looked Joe College cool. Plus, the guys he hung out with were *the* guys.

Jeff, in a word, was a hunk: six-foot-two-inches tall, with the broad shoulders of a swimmer, which he was in high school and college. Jeff's streaky blond hair and blue eyes turned my knees to jelly. We had a great evening, and when he asked me for my phone number, I wrote it down with eyeliner on his right arm.

The next day he called me, and we spent every waking moment together until he had to go back to the university for the second semester. On one of our early dates, he bought me a pair of jeans, and then he escorted me to a series of really nice restaurants—each spiffier than the one the night before. I was wined and dined big time, but what really impressed me—and you're going to laugh when you read this—is that he had a cell phone in his car. Hey, this was 1989, and cell phones were a big deal!

When Jeff introduced me to his parents, I realized things were happening really fast. *He could be the one,* I thought. What about that list of qualities that I had written down when I was younger? Who needed to look at *that?* I was in *love.* And I was to learn later that I was blind.

I'm going to scrunch together a lot of details here, but over the next three years, we dated hot and heavy, and when people get hot and heavy, two things usually happen:

1. You can get too physical.
2. You start talking about marriage.

I'll talk about the physical part in chapter 5, but the

marriage part was as inevitable as the next moonrise, as far as we were concerned. I planned to become Mrs. Jeff Taylor one day.

In October 1993, Jeff asked me to marry him, and I said yes. We set a tentative date that we agreed we would work toward: December 3, 1994. That seemed like enough time to plan a proper wedding.

The reason I'm telling you all this is because of what happened over the next few months. Whenever Jeff and I discussed what church we would get married in, it set off the biggest row. I wanted to get married in my Southern Baptist church; Jeff insisted that we would be getting married in his Roman Catholic church. Slowly it was dawning on me: Our different backgrounds, our different ways of relating to God and worshiping the Creator of the universe, made a difference. I had convinced myself that those differences didn't matter, but they did.

Jeff and I tried to work it out—we even went to counseling—but when it came down to it, I realized how much my religious tradition meant to me. As I wavered, Jeff demonstrated that he was getting the proverbial cold feet as well; he informed me that he could not commit to the December date. When I asked what date he could commit to, he talked in circles about getting married "sometime in the future."

Within a week I made the very difficult decision to break the engagement, the hardest thing I had ever done in my life because I was not a quitter. But we had to call off the wedding. I sobbed for days and thought my world had ended.

During that time of introspection, however, I rediscovered that Qualities List I mentioned earlier. At the very top was this attribute: spiritual compatibility.

Bingo.

I was trying to push the square peg of my Southern Baptist upbringing into the round hole of Jeff's Roman Catholic background. I was not on the same spiritual wavelength as my future husband, and the more I thought about it, the more I realized how important my spiritual heritage was to me.

Then I looked at the second item on my Qualities List that said, "Clear direction in life." In other words, I didn't want to hitch my wagon to someone who was wavering on the Biggest Decision Ever.

MICHAEL SAYS

I'm so glad that Amy realized she needed to back out of her relationship with Jeff. And I'm also happy that she found her Qualities List and began to take it seriously.

We can all look back and wish we had done things differently. I wish I had known about making a Qualities List before I started my dating career, which began in junior high and motored right into college at Baylor University, where I met Amy. We were both members of the Baylor yell squad—the cheerleaders who pumped up crowds at Bear football and basketball games and who performed stunts such as lifts and flips.

Amy's list was important because by the time we started dating, several months after she broke off her wedding engagement, she *knew* what she wanted out of a dating relationship. She told me from the get-go that she wasn't dating to mess around but to determine if our relationship would go the distance.

We both believe it's a great idea to make a Qualities List before a relationship heats up. Now would be a great time to do some levelheaded thinking. If you've never made a list, it's not that hard. We've provided some space at the end of the chapter for you to make your list. Or you could keep the list on your computer. But before you write anything down, let's talk about a few things.

We know which quality should be number one on your list: The person you date should be a Christian. It doesn't do either person any good when a Christian and a non-Christian get into a dating relationship, because it's not going to work out for the long term. Sure, it's easy to say, "He'll become a Christian after spending some time with me!" In our experiences working with young people, however, it's often the Christians who see their spiritual lives suffer. They feel pressured to make compromises because non-Christians do not have a biblical worldview regarding premarital sex, the importance of going to church, and reading the Bible.

God's Word is also very clear about the dangers of

Christians and non-Christians hooking up. A New Testament passage asks: "How can a believer be a partner with an unbeliever?" (2 Corinthians 6:15). This is what's known as being "unequally yoked," a farming term from the old days when two oxen plowing a field were joined by a wooden bar around their necks to keep them pulling the plow in unison. If you joined a donkey and an ox with a yoke, you'd be yelling "Whoa, Nellie" a lot because the animals could not work together since one animal is taller and wider than the other. Nope, you don't want to become romantically involved with a non-Christian.

If that is the number one quality on your list, what are the others? Before you write anything more, think about the four pieces of clothing you need in order to be well dressed for a dating relationship:

- Robe of prayer
- Belt of accountability
- Shoes of honor
- Shield of purity

How does your dating partner measure up to the dress code? Does he or she have an active prayer life, praying about important decisions? Is he or she involved in accountability relationships? Is your dating partner respectful and gracious? Is he or she committed to sexual purity? These are foundational qualities you would want in a dating partner—not to mention a marriage partner.

What about the four things you put on your mental list when we asked you some questions at the beginning of the chapter? Do they go on your list somewhere?

As you fill out the rest of your list, consider these qualities:

Qualities That Would Be Good in a Guy

- *He has a heart for God.* What's his walk with Christ like? Does he take it seriously? Does he drag his feet to church? Has he been part of a Bible study? Is he still in one?

- *He has a heart for people.* How does he treat others in your presence? Is he rude to wait staff? Does he look down on parking attendants? Or does he have a great heart for people he runs into?

- *He has a cheerful heart.* Is he moody? Is he the silent type? Is he fun to be around?

- *He has a sense of humor.* Does he make you laugh? Or is he as dull as typing out a term paper? Can you make him laugh?

- *He comes from a good family.* Does it appear that he was raised in a loving, intact household where family members treat each other with respect? Remember: you will probably be treated the same way as his father treats his mother. Is that a good thing or a bad thing? No matter how much we pretend otherwise, parents are role models.

- *He's accepting of who you are.* Some guys like to make cutting asides about your weight ("Still packing the freshman fifteen?") or your roommates ("That Caroline is a real Froot Loop."). What could he really be thinking about you?

- *He's willing to wait.* Sure, the hormones are churning like a Mixmaster but is he willing to respect your (and—we hope—his) boundaries? Does he paw you when you kiss, letting his hands and fingers work their way toward places they shouldn't go? Flat out, has he told you that he's a virgin and made a commitment to wait to have sex until he's married?

- *He knows who he is and where he's going.* Does he convey a winner's attitude? What are his career aspirations? Do those coincide at all with yours?

- *He's realistic about the future.* Some guys pursue vain goals, like Don Quixote, who rode with his lance at full tilt against a row of windmills, which he had mistaken for evil giants. Does your beau talk about taking over Microsoft and evicting Bill Gates from his 40,000 square- foot mansion in the moneyed Seattle suburb of Medina?

- *He has similar interests.* If you like to ride a touring bicycle every afternoon, while his idea of free time is playing the latest Madden NFL game on his Sony PlayStation2 console, you probably don't have the same recreational goals. What do you like to do together?

- *He's willing to watch "chick flicks."* You don't want to spend the rest of your life watching the latest James

Bond thriller or *Dumb and Dumber* on video for the forty-ninth time, do you? You want someone who also appreciates the emotions behind well-crafted love stories and tear-jerker plot lines.

- *He's attractive.* This is the last quality on our list, which doesn't mean it's not important. In the long term, physical looks are one part of the combination plate, not the whole enchilada. Sure, a gorgeous hunk with killer abs and blue eyes counts for something, but beauty is only skin deep. What's his beauty like underneath the gift wrapping?

Qualities That Would Be Good in a Girl

- *She loves the Lord.* Is she on the same page as you regarding her faith? Does she attend church regularly and read her Bible? Is her faith real, or is she just playing along?

- *She has a great personality.* Do you find her fun to be around? What are her mood swings like? Can you tell she's working overtime not to exhibit what could charitably be called her PMS?

- *She has a clear direction in life.* What are her long-range plans? Is she on a career track? Looking forward to marrying someday and having a family?

- *She reaches out to others.* Is she an introvert or an extrovert? How does she interact with others? You can often learn about this trait when you go on double dates or go out bowling with another couple, for example.

- *She comes from a good family.* How do her family members interact with each other? Do they encourage each other and treat each other with respect? Do they want what's best for the other? How is her relationship with her father? Her security and the way she relates to men is often tied up in that father-daughter relationship.

- *She is willing to watch action movies.* You don't want to spend the rest of your life watching only those "chick flick" movies, do you? You want someone who also appreciates the artistry behind car chases and gun shoot-outs.

- *She respects herself.* Not all the sexual aggressors in the world these days are male. This message comes with a 100 percent guarantee: If a young woman makes herself sexually available to you, you won't be able to resist more than a couple of times. And you can take that to the bank.

- *She is cute and thumps your attraction buttons.* Is she beautiful to you? Do you feel as though she lights up a room when she walks over to meet you?

AMY SAYS I had just graduated from Baylor University when I broke off my engagement to Jeff. Talk about turmoil in my life! My best-laid plans—to graduate from college, get married, buy a home with a white picket fence, and wait for the kids to arrive—was tossed into the air like confetti. Suddenly, I was single again. It didn't take long for word to get around my hometown of Conroe, Texas, that Amy Renée Johnston was "available" again.

I went out with several guys, but Michael Smalley, one of my good friends on the Baylor cheer team, kept hovering in my thoughts. I decided to try something different: I began praying for God to bring the right person into my life. I didn't know whether that would be Michael, but I was tired of trying to go my own way and have the Lord play catch-up in my life. This time, I wanted God to orchestrate my love life.

So I prayed. Read my Bible. Asked God to lead me, whatever the future held.

Michael knew that I was available following the breakup, but he had flown to Mazatlan, Mexico, to participate in a six-week Baylor study-abroad summer program to shore up his Spanish requirements. The program ended in mid- July.

I later learned that Michael's prayer time with God was never as rich as it was while he was in Mazatlan. He, too, was praying that the Lord would bring someone special into his life. He told me later that he felt it would be me because we were such good friends at Baylor, but he didn't want to presume that God didn't have someone better. But he sure liked me a lot.

That attraction was manifested by the hour-long phone calls and lovesick poetry that I received from Mazatlan. You could say that this is when we really first got to know each other, which shows that relationships don't always have to start with a dinner and a movie. I began praying about Michael, asking God for direction and peace for whatever happened between us. I know it sounds crazy to say this, but I felt as if the Lord was showing me that Michael and I would one day minister together—talking to young people about topics like dating and not having premarital sex.

I had a pretty strong feeling that Michael would ask me out when he returned from Mexico. At this point in my life, I was ready. I didn't want to play around and be in a relationship just to say that I was in a relationship.

Let's see. How long was I home from Mazatlan before I picked up a phone and asked Amy whether she would like to come visit me?

I think it was fifteen minutes. Maybe twenty, but it couldn't have been much longer. When I called her, I was all bubbly because I was back in the United States and could drink the water again and not deal with turista. I told Amy how things were hopping in Branson, a resort area that caters to tens of thousands of tourists with dozens of great family-oriented shows.

"There's a lot happening in Branson," I said over the phone. "You should come up here and check it out. Maybe we could go to a show."

"I would love to do that," Amy responded, and that's when our relationship passed Go.

The following weekend, I picked up Amy at the Springfield/Branson Regional Airport and took her to my parents' home, where she stayed in our guest room. For the next few days, we had a blast going to the local water park, hitting the Branson outlet stores, and dining out in romantic restaurants.

As Amy and I discussed the six-week period that we both prayed and waited, we realized that God had been faithful to answer our prayers. God knows what is best for us. And because we were confident that he had brought us together, we could move ahead confidently in our relationship.

In fact, I wanted to get married right away, but I waited a few months to ask her to become my bride,

Top ten reasons why he or she *might not* be the best date for you

10. He insists that his mother drives you on dates.

9. She eats hamburgers with a fork and knife.

8. He uses your hair as dental floss.

7. She owns more Mary Kay products than Mary Kay herself.

6. He picks his teeth with his comb.

5. She says she needs to get the same style of shoes—but in a different color.

4. His idea of a romantic Saturday night is shooting pool at Billy Bob's Bar and Grill.

3. When she makes spaghetti, she substitutes ketchup for tomato sauce.

2. His mother still comes over once a week to iron his underwear.

1. You didn't know her real first name was Always . . . as in Always Right.

and she accepted my proposal. We married in the middle of December, less than six months from our first date.

We realized later that was too soon, because we discovered in our first year of marriage that we had to get over a few hurdles—mainly stemming from her relationship with Jeff. But we made it through that painful time, and I think it's because we began our relationship with prayer and a godly foundation that undergirded our lives.

So, we are giving you two assignments: First, if you aren't already doing it, start to pray about the person God wants you to date—and possibly marry. Put on the robe of prayer. And pray about everything. Nothing is off-limits for prayer. Pray not only about leading you to the person God wants you to date and possibly marry but also about becoming the person God wants you to be; he may be preparing you for someone too.

The second assignment is this: Fill out your Qualities List, outlining what you would want to see in someone you date. Keep the list in this book or on your computer so that you can quickly refer to it. Then remember to consult the list. Don't make the mistake Amy did.

Guys tend not to make out Qualities Lists. I understand; I didn't either. It's taken more than a few reminders from me to get the guys in my youth group to make out their Qualities List. Take a few moments now, and get this done. Doing so could save you years of grief, all for the investment of less than a half hour.

If you've been praying about your dating and have started

a Qualities List, you've begun to dress for a successful dating relationship. As you meet people, however, realize that people have different personalities. We'll talk more about how our personalities come into play in our next chapter.

My Qualities List

What qualities am I looking for in a dating partner—and eventually a marriage partner?

1. _____

2. _____

3. _____

4. _____

5. _____

6. _____

7. _____

8. _____

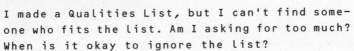

Dear Mike & Amy,

I made a Qualities List, but I can't find someone who fits the list. Am I asking for too much? When is it okay to ignore the list?

—Just wondering

YOU'VE ASKED SOME IMPORTANT QUESTIONS. WE'LL TRY TO ANSWER THE SECOND QUESTION FIRST. FIGURE OUT WHAT ITEMS ON YOUR LIST ARE NONNEGOTIABLES. WE SUGGEST THAT FINDING SOMEONE WHO'S A CHRISTIAN IS SOMETHING YOU SHOULD NOT COMPROMISE ABOUT. THAT'S A KEY ISSUE. REMEMBER MY (AMY'S) STORY IN THIS CHAPTER: I HAD "SPIRITUAL COMPATIBILITY" ON MY LIST, BUT I IGNORED IT IN A SIGNIFICANT RELATIONSHIP, AND THE RESULT WAS LOTS OF PAIN AND REGRET.

BESIDES THE SPIRITUAL ISSUES, WHAT ARE YOUR NONNEGOTIABLES? WE SUGGEST THAT YOU HOLD OUT IN YOUR SEARCH FOR FOUNDATIONAL QUALITIES LIKE HONOR, RESPECT, AND UNCONDITIONAL LOVE. IN THE LONG RUN, YOU WOULD NOT WANT TO INVEST IN A SERIOUS RELATIONSHIP THAT COULD LEAD TO MARRIAGE IF THE PERSON LACKED THESE QUALITIES. HOWEVER, IF YOU CAN'T FIND SOMEONE WHO SHARES YOUR LOVE FOR MARIAH CAREY OR WHITE-WATER RAFTING OR THE LAKERS, YOU CAN PROBABLY LIVE WITH THOSE DIFFERENCES.

AS FOR THE FIRST QUESTION—AM I ASKING FOR TOO MUCH?—YOU ARE THE BEST JUDGE OF THAT. IT'S NOT WRONG TO WANT THE RIGHT PERSON, BUT IF YOU HAVE A TENDENCY TO BE A PERFECTIONIST, THAT MAY MAKE IT NEARLY IMPOSSIBLE FOR SOMEONE TO MEET YOUR EXPECTATIONS. MANY TIMES OUR EXPECTATIONS OF OTHERS ARE A REFLECTION OF WHAT WE EXPECT FROM OURSELVES. SO OUR RECOMMENDATION WOULD BE TO IDENTIFY THE NONNEGOTIABLES AND STICK TO THOSE. THEN RELAX. TRY TO ACCEPT SOME OF YOUR OWN IMPERFECTIONS. YOU MIGHT BE SURPRISED WHO POPS INTO YOUR LIFE WHEN YOU DON'T PUT SO MUCH PRESSURE ON YOURSELF.

—Mike & Amy

Dear Mike & Amy,

I want to be a good husband someday. How can I prepare now for that? How can I build character and work on qualities that will show women that I date that I will be a good (godly) husband?

—Wants to prepare

Dear Wants to Prepare,

We know many girls who would be thrilled to hear a guy ask this question. Just the fact that you want to be a godly husband says a lot about you.

As for character qualities, we've already mentioned some in this chapter. A big one in our book is honor. Does your dating partner see you honoring others above yourself (see Romans 12:10)? Do you show honor to her? Do you resist belittling her and others? Do you listen with respect to other people's opinions? If so, you're a long way down the path of becoming a godly husband for someone. If not, ask God to give you the ability to show honor.

An important quality in becoming a godly husband is having a deep relationship with the Lord now. Do you pray about your decisions? Do you regularly study the Bible? Do you submit your will to God?

What about integrity? Trust is such a key factor in any relationship, but especially in a marriage. Are you trustworthy? Are you a man of your word? Does who you say you are line up with who you really are? Are you dependable and honest? If your girlfriend sees you fudging on little stuff now, how would she be able to trust you as a husband? Now is the time to begin a relationship built on trust.

One of the New Testament pictures of a husband's role with his wife is one who loves her self-sacrificially, just as Christ gave his life for his bride, the church (see Ephesians 5:21-33). Are you self-

SACRIFICIAL IN YOUR DATING RELATIONSHIP, OR MUST
YOU ALWAYS CALL THE SHOTS AND HAVE YOUR OWN WAY? DO
YOU THINK OF THE NEEDS OF YOUR GIRLFRIEND FIRST?
ARE YOU UNDERSTANDING, THOUGHTFUL, AND KIND?

WE ADMIRE YOUR WISH TO BE A GODLY PERSON. WE PRAY
THAT GOD WILL SHOW YOU THE WAY AND HELP YOU FIND A
YOUNG WOMAN WHO WILL BE A GODLY WIFE FOR YOU.

—Mike & Amy

Dear Mike & Amy,

I'm a twenty-two-year-old female who's been dating various guys for six years. I haven't found a
Christian that I think would make a good husband. I'm currently dating a guy who's thoughtful, kind, sacrificial, respectful of my
boundaries, good with kids, and lots of fun to be
around. However, he's not a Christian. Should I
be concerned about that, or can I assume that
somewhere along the way he will see the light and
give himself to Christ?

—Optimistic

DEAR OPTIMISTIC,

OH, DEAR SISTER, WE FEEL YOUR PAIN. YOU FOUND MR.
RIGHT BUT WITH JUST A LITTLE BIT OF MR. WRONG. THE
COLD FACTS ARE THAT RESEARCH INDICATES THAT LACK OF
RELIGIOUS AGREEMENT IS ONE OF THE BEST PREDICTORS
OF DIVORCE. HOWARD MARKMAN, A DEAR FRIEND AND RE-
SPECTED RESEARCHER OF WHY COUPLES DIVORCE, WOULD
STRONGLY CAUTION YOU TO SERIOUSLY TAKE ANOTHER
LOOK AROUND. REMEMBER WHAT WE SAID EARLIER IN THIS
CHAPTER: IF TWO PEOPLE ARE "UNEQUALLY YOKED,"
THERE IS ALWAYS GOING TO BE A RUB BECAUSE OF THE

DIFFERENCES. IF YOU MARRY THIS GUY, YOU WILL POSSI-
BLY DEVELOP BLISTERS WHERE YOUR FAITH AND HIS LACK
OF FAITH RUB. OVER TIME THE BLISTERS BECOME CAL-
LUSES—MEANING EITHER YOU BECOME LESS SENSITIVE IN
YOUR RELATIONSHIP WITH YOUR HUSBAND OR YOU BECOME
LESS SENSITIVE TO GOD'S DIRECTION.

DATING A NON-CHRISTIAN IN THE HOPE THAT HE OR SHE
WILL SEE THE LIGHT HAS "NOBLE GESTURE" WRITTEN ALL
OVER IT, BUT WHAT OFTEN HAPPENS WHEN CHRISTIANS AND
NON-CHRISTIANS DATE IS THAT THE CHRISTIAN'S SPIRI-
TUAL LIFE SUFFERS. IT HAS TO! YOU'RE MIXING LIGHT
WITH DARKNESS. IT'S BETTER TO REMAIN "JUST
FRIENDS," BUT YOU CAN CERTAINLY MAKE THE INTRODUC-
TION TO CHRIST BY ASKING HIM TO JOIN YOU AT CHURCH.
CONTINUE TO PRAY FOR HIM, BUT WE ENCOURAGE YOU TO
DISENGAGE FROM THE DATING RELATIONSHIP.

—Mike & Amy

3
it's all in your personality

MICHAEL SAYS

Two months after Amy and I began dating, I was ready to make my move. I can't tell you how crazy I was about her, how excited I was to be in her presence, and how much I contemplated what it would be like to be married to her and wake up in the morning next to her.

But there was one thing I had to know about Amy. If she would agree to my proposition, then nothing would stand in the way between us and the altar.

"Amy?" I casually said one evening as we munched on nachos at El Chico, a great Tex-Mex joint a block from the Baylor University campus.

"Yes, Michael?" Amy looked at me with doe-like eyes of wonder and sensed that I was ready to pop The Question.

"Amy, I was wondering if . . ." I couldn't finish my thought. It was too important, too tied in with the future of our relationship.

"Michael, it's fine," she said, as she reached and took my hand in hers. "You can ask me anything."

"Thank you, Amy," I said as I made a grab for another

mouthful of cheese-and-bean nachos. "What I was wondering was if you would be interested in . . . in going rock climbing with me?"

"Rock climbing? That sounds like fun."

"Have you ever been rock climbing before?"

"No, but I'd love to try."

I exhaled a huge breath because I was stoked. "That's great, Amy. I thought we could drive over to Shandon Rock this weekend and climb with some of my buddies. I'm sure it will be a lot of fun."

A few days later I held the belay rope as Amy attacked a series of bridge walls along the Brazos River. She didn't exactly scamper up those sheer cliffs like Spider-Woman, but she never whined about getting twenty, thirty, forty feet off the ground. Her coast-to-coast grin told me that she was having a *great* time.

That day of rock climbing was huge to me because high on my list of qualities was someone who was not fearful. Amy was adventurous because that quality fits her personality.

Did I say *personality?*

I love talking about personality traits because it's such a fascinating subject. Your personality, as any Psych 101 prof would tell you on the first day of class, is a combination of traits that you were born with. These personality traits subconsciously affect how you think and how you act.

Have you ever wondered why you do the things that you do? Have you ever wondered why you get along with some people and not with others? Do you ever wonder why certain friends rub you the wrong way or why some people are so obnoxious?

It's often tied to our personalities. The study of psychology has narrowed down human behavior into four basic personality—or temperament—types. My brother, Greg, and I (along with a friend named Bob Paul) came up with four names to describe them, and they're based on the leadership team that you would find on a cruise ship. Imagine *The Princess Seas* leaving port. What would you need to have a successful cruise?

Answer: a Captain, a Social Director, a Navigator, and a Steward. These four persons mirror each of the four basic personality types that we could be. Let's take a closer look at each one:

Captains are the leader types. They are usually the bosses at work. They act decisively and are sure of themselves. They are doers—not the type of folks who sit around and wait for things to happen. Captains love to solve problems and fix things. They are blunt, bottom-line people. The downside of this personality is that Captains can come across as insensitive at times. They are the types who boast about walking over their own grandmas if that's what it would take to close a deal, win an election, or be victorious on the field. If Captains are not put in charge, they will figure out a way to get themselves in charge. Captains' communication style is direct and one-way; they are not known for being good listeners.

Social Directors are the fun-loving types who are great networkers. They seem to know everybody, and they're always up for a party—because then they get to know more people! Social Directors are great at motivating others ("C'mon, let's go down to the beach! We'll have a blast!") and getting things on the calendar. They want everybody to like them, and they are usually well liked because of their contagious enthusiasm and inspiration. On the downside, they tend to avoid details, and they daydream a lot. That often makes them as disorganized as an absent-minded professor. Because they crave social recognition and approval by the group, they tend to walk on the edge, which sometimes leads to some inappropriate behavior. Social directors' communication style is one-way because of their high energy.

Stewards are the warm and relational types who are so loyal that if you told them to get lost, they would tell all their friends what a great person you are. Stewards enjoy routine to the point that they don't mind staying in a rut. On the downside, they often absorb emotional pain and punishment in relationships because that's their nature— loyalty ranks high. But watch out: if you get on their bad side, they hurt easily and can nurse a grudge until the Second Coming. That's why stewards can be the world's greatest procrastinators. Stewards' communication style is two-way because they are great listeners, but they talk too long and get bogged down in too many details.

Navigators are the quality-control types who've got to do

things "by the book." They will even read Microsoft Word user guides! Navigators are forever analyzing things because they love being accurate and precise. Rules are big with them, but they are often too critical and too negative regarding new opportunities. They rarely appear in public with a hair out of place, and if you peeked inside their bedrooms, you would find a clean desk, a made bed, and all the clothes hung up—possibly with all the blue shirts hanging together and everything else color coordinated. Navigators' communication style is two-way, but they can drive you crazy asking about details.

I'm really glad I knew this stuff when I met Amy. I might not have had my Qualities List tucked away in my wallet, but I knew in my head that I wanted to go out with and eventually marry a Navigator with some Social Director in her. That's because I'm a high Social Director with a bit of a Captain in me. I needed someone to complement me, someone who was detail oriented and could keep me on task but could also loosen up and get crazy with me. And not be fearful if I wanted to jump off a cliff and into a roaring river.

After Amy and I married, it took her about two days to notice that I had a habit of shedding clothes when I came home from work. As soon as I stepped inside the front door, I dropped sweaters and shirts and slipped off shoes and pants as I trekked from the living room to the master bedroom. Amy, as the quality-control Navigator, didn't appreciate this idiosyncrasy in my character. Something had to be done because I didn't like to hear her criticism. Since we understood our differing personality quirks, we worked out a system where I promised not to change out of my clothes unless I was standing in *my* walk-in closet (she has her own). I still didn't hang up and put away my clothes immediately, but at least this kept the clothes-on-the-floor pattern restricted to a part of the house that the public never saw.

AMY SAYS

I'm glad I understood Michael and where he was coming from before we got married, but he sure walked to the beat of a different drummer. He didn't mind dirty dishes stacking up on kitchen counters; I liked everything rinsed and put away in the dishwasher right away. Michael's idea of cleaning the car was passing through one of those quick-wash places and air drying the car by driving fast on the highway; I liked my cars to be spotless, which meant I washed them regularly and swabbed the air conditioning vents with Q-Tips.

I had a good handle on Michael's quirky personality because he asked me to take a personality profile test shortly after we began dating. (We strongly urge you and your boyfriend or girlfriend to take our personality profile test, which you can find on the Internet by going to www.smalleyonline.com. Click on "Online Enrichment," then under "Online Relationship Testing" click on "personality test." The test is free, so you have no excuse not to take it.)

You'll be asked to identify the degree to which certain characteristics or behaviors most accurately describe you. The scale is:

0 = not at all
1 = somewhat
2 = mostly
3 = very much

For instance, you'll grade yourself on how optimistic you are or whether you see yourself as a perfectionist. After you've graded yourself on sixty-four characteristics, you'll click a button, and within seconds, you'll have your own report. It's fun—unless you're a Navigator like me, because we painstakingly take our time completing tests. Michael, the Social Director that he is, raced through his test, but that was okay because there are no wrong and no right answers in the Smalley personality profile test. It's just a tool that points out the *tendencies* that you display in your personality. If you can get your dating partner to take the test, the two of you can compare notes and learn something about your strengths and weaknesses. After you've clicked on the red dot to get your column totals and recorded them, be sure to click on the link to the personality interpretations. The strengths and weaknesses described there could help you.

MICHAEL SAYS

I absolutely love talking to young people about personality types. Young women often ask me what a male Captain looks like. My reply is that a male Captain is the guy who likes to lead the parade, the one who enjoys being in charge. He surrounds himself with buddies who are Stewards; they are loyal and tell him what a great guy he is. Captains can be loud and brash, kind of like hotheaded linebackers on the football team. Women are often unaware that Captains have trouble being sensitive, so if you're easily offended or hurt, you need to be aware of that.

It's difficult for a male and a female Captain to date each other—each one wants to be holding the reins and controlling where the relationship goes. They will even have a tough time agreeing on what pizza topping to get. Captains who date each other often break up because they keep tripping over each other's egos.

Male Navigators are usually good students who make high grades in classes I was never good in—math and science. They excel at nearly everything they do, but they like staying in the background. They are great listeners.

Male Social Directors are the life of the party, the guys with a fast smile and a quick hello for you. They do all sorts of sports and extracurricular activities, like band and theater. At concerts, they are always the crazy guys going nuts in the mosh pit, although they would prefer to be on-stage and working the crowd into a frenzy because they want to make sure everyone is having a good time. *Bring in the clowns.* I was the class clown, hands down. Amy loves that in me because she knows that I will keep life interesting. No dull weekends playing Parcheesi for us. Life has to happen!

A guy Steward is sensitive and caring, and he loves children. (A Captain or a Navigator, on the other hand, often ignores children.) Stewards prefer to watch concerts from a distance instead of mixing it up in front of the stage—and don't ask him to get near a microphone! If you're dating a male Steward, you will have to draw him out. You may even have to maneuver him to ask you out. You should be prepared to take more of a lead in the relationship.

Again, please know that people can be combinations of these four predominant character traits and that there is nothing "wrong" with any of them; it's just who we are. Although I'm the Social Director type, I have some Captain and some Steward in my genes. Therefore, since I enjoy being in charge, I cast myself as a sweet leader. People recognized those qualities in me, because I was not only the captain of the football team, captain of the basketball team, and student body president, but I also started a fraternity. I fit into those leadership roles well, and I enjoyed them.

But what does a Captain look like in a female? Very much like a guy Captain. Girl Captains will be very strong and opinionated, and they won't take any you-know-what from anybody. They won't back down in an argument, and they will react negatively if they feel they are getting a raw deal. You might not want to talk too much about the role of "submission" in a relationship with a female Captain. She'll bite your head off, as if to say, *You got that wrong, buddy.*

Amy definitely is the Navigator/Social Director type, but she has some Captain in her. She would be unhappy if she were a stay-at-home mom all the time; she needs a career on the side. She loves going on speaking tours with me and counseling others. That's because female Navigators are intense, fact-oriented women. If you are looking to date a young woman who would want to be a stay-at-home mom, who would thrive in that role and be content with building a nest, then you don't want to date a Captain.

You might be better off dating a Steward, who is more of a nest builder. Most women enjoy that role, to a certain extent, but some enjoy it more than others. Stewards are sensitive to others' feelings and often serve as peacemakers in conflict. They can be great listeners, but they are often shy.

An important point to make here is that there are not major gender differences between a male Social Director and a female one, for instance. Amy and I socialize with our good friends Shawn and Christina Stover, and Christina and I are identical Social Directors: totally off the wall, like to get crazy, and don't give us directions to find someone else's home. Oh, and did I tell you that Christina and I were born to shop?

The same goes for Captains, Stewards, whatever. If you flip around the channels on a Sunday morning, you'll come across a female preacher, a Captain if I ever saw one. She'll be in total command, preaching exactly like her male counterparts with an intense delivery punctuated by raising and lowering her voice and jabbing the air with her hands to make a point.

The next time you go to a football game, check out the cheerleaders. *No, I don't mean that way.* Check them out, and see if you can see all four personality types in a cheerleading squad. The Captains will be the ones out front, trying to get the crowd to go nuts after a big play. The Captains of the yell team are . . . well, captains. It's that simple.

The Social Directors are in the second row, but they aren't trying to get the crowd to go nuts. Instead, they're acting nuts themselves, jumping around and having a good time. Social Directors are happy if everyone is having a good time. They are the party animals.

Steward cheerleaders are role players. They, too, love what they're doing, but they are usually the base of a pyramid, holding other cheerleaders up. Navigator cheerleaders are more concerned that the stunts and cheers are done correctly. You can see them concentrating and counting off their movements because everything has to be done correctly. They like predictability.

AMY
SAYS

I can hear the gears turning. You're probably wondering, *What are some good pairings with these personality types?* Before we go much further, have you gone to our Web site and taken the test? If so, good. With that information in hand, here are two pairings that Michael and I believe would be good matches:

- Captains and Stewards
- Social Directors and Navigators

Please keep in mind several things. Most people are not *all* Captain or *all* Social Director. There's a little mix involved, but what we're talking about is when one of the four traits is *predominant*. This doesn't mean that two Captains couldn't have a successful relationship: in Washington, D.C., they are known as "power couples." In high school, it's the starting quarterback dating the captain of the yell squad.

But two Captains or two Navigators? That's going to take a lot of work. Two Social Directors shouldn't hook up, either; they would be too all-over-the-map to get it together. They would have a ton of fun together, but they are the type that if they got together to study, they wouldn't get a lick done!

Interestingly enough, Stewards have a personality type that could be a good match with almost anyone. They are peaceful, easygoing, and relaxing to be around. Nothing fazes them. They like a normal routine, which can be a big help to a Social Director who's panicking because she's late—she's always, always late.

If you're hearing this personality stuff for the first time, I would not be surprised if you thought this sounds bizarre. Hang in there. The sooner you get on to it, the sooner you can put these principles into practice. Michael and I believe that the best relationships shouldn't happen by accident.

Dear Mike & Amy,

I'm a female who's nearly twenty. Is it all right for me to ask a guy out, or do I have to wait until some guy asks me?

—Eager to date

DEAR EAGER TO DATE,

AH, THAT'S A GREAT QUESTION IN THE POSTFEMINIST AGE WE LIVE IN, BUT OUR ANSWER IS AS TRADITIONAL AS A THREE-TIERED WEDDING CAKE: IT'S THE GUY WHO MUST MAKE THE CALL.

HAVING A GIRL ASK HIM OUT EMASCULATES A YOUNG MALE, AND THAT'S NOT A GOOD THING FOR THE LONG-TERM FUTURE OF THE RELATIONSHIP. TEACHER AND COUNSELOR JOHN ELDREDGE, WRITING IN *WILD AT HEART*, SAID, "SOCIETY AT LARGE CAN'T MAKE UP ITS MIND ABOUT MEN. HAVING SPENT THE LAST THIRTY YEARS REDEFINING MASCULINITY INTO SOMETHING MORE SENSITIVE, SAFE, MANAGEABLE AND, WELL, FEMININE, IT NOW BERATES MEN FOR NOT BEING MEN" (PP. 6–7).

GUYS, IN THEIR MASCULINE ROLES, NEED TO BE PURSUERS. THIS DOESN'T MEAN THAT A YOUNG WOMAN CANNOT BE EQUALLY INVOLVED IN PLANNING DATES AND HAVING FUN, BUT SHE SHOULD WAIT TO BE ASKED OUT.

IF YOU HAVE IN MIND A SPECIFIC GUY WHOM YOU WOULD LIKE TO ASK YOU OUT, TRY TO MAKE HIM FEEL COMFORTABLE AROUND YOU. MAKE HIM LAUGH. LAUGHTER IS THE BEST ICEBREAKER; IT MAKES EVERYONE FEEL MORE COMFORTABLE. IF YOU SENSE HE'S SHY, THEN YOU MIGHT WANT TO MAKE A JOKE ABOUT A DUMB MISTAKE YOU MADE AT WORK (OR SOMETHING IN THE CONTEXT OF THE SITUATION YOU BOTH SHARE). BY SHOWING A LITTLE HUMILITY, YOU LET HIM KNOW YOU'RE HUMAN.

—Mike & Amy

Dear Mike & Amy,

I'm a nineteen-year-old female, and I'd like to begin dating. How do I start?

—Needs help

DEAR NEEDS HELP,

THE FIRST PLACE TO START IS TAKING INVENTORY ON YOURSELF. ASK YOURSELF A FEW QUESTIONS: WHY DO I WANT TO DATE? AM I READY TO GIVE AND RECEIVE IN A RELATIONSHIP?

MANY TIMES WE DATE JUST TO HAVE SOMEONE IN OUR LIFE TO DO THINGS WITH OR SO WE LOOK BETTER TO OUR FRIENDS. THIS IS SHALLOW DATING—AND FOR ONE OR TWO DATES THAT'S FINE. BUT IF THAT'S ALL YOU'RE READY FOR, DON'T LEAD THE GUY ON. WHAT I MEAN BY THAT IS DON'T GO OUT WITH HIM MORE THAN THREE TIMES. (AND IT DOESN'T MATTER IF YOU TELL THE PERSON, "OH, I'M NOT READY FOR A RELATIONSHIP. IS THAT OKAY WITH YOU?" BY CONTINUING TO GO OUT WITH THAT PERSON, YOU ARE SENDING MIXED MESSAGES.)

BUT IT SOUNDS AS IF YOU ARE READY TO DIVE IN. WHEN SERIOUSLY THINKING ABOUT DATING, MAKE A LIST OF THE QUALITIES YOU FEEL ARE THE MOST IMPORTANT TO YOU IN A HUSBAND—THE KIND OF QUALITIES THAT WILL LAST FOR

A LIFETIME. THEN LOOK FOR GUYS WHO APPEAR TO HAVE THOSE QUALITIES. SOME QUALITIES ARE NOT SO OBVIOUS IMMEDIATELY, BUT YOU CAN GET A GENERAL SENSE ABOUT A PERSON. SECOND—AND I WISH SOMEONE WOULD HAVE TOLD ME THIS—LOOK AT YOUR PERSONALITY, AND THINK ABOUT WHAT KIND OF GUY COMPLEMENTS YOU BEST. FOR EXAMPLE, BECAUSE MICHAEL IS SO FUN AND OUTGOING, HE ENCOURAGES ME TO BE LESS SERIOUS. I NEED THAT.

—Amy

4
dating 101

We've all had embarrassing dating experiences. Remember how my dating life started with Stacy—watermelon-on-the-face Stacy?

It's not all bad to have a few embarrassing situations while you're dating. It gives you a chance to see how the two of you react under certain kinds of pressure. In that restaurant, when I wanted nothing more than to disappear and die, Stacy proved to be gracious, forgiving, and fun. That embarrassing night was the beginning of a great dating relationship.

Stacy and I dated every weekend, and during the week we talked on the phone. We sat next to each other at youth group, school, lunch, you name it; we were everywhere together.

This may sound like a heavy dating relationship to you. In many ways, it was. But my parents allowed me to see Stacy because I showed her respect. Stacy and I never got into trouble physically because I respected her limits, which were mine as well. If we had been kissing for several minutes and she felt things were getting a tad too warm, she would say, "Hey, let's stop," or "We better slow down." There was mutual accountability going on.

Stacy and I, I'm proud to say, had a healthy dating experience. I learned a great deal about self-confidence at a time when I viewed myself as a dork. I loved the interaction with someone of the opposite sex, and those experiences proved invaluable when I began going out with the person I would eventually marry—Amy Johnston.

AMY SAYS

That's right. Michael was a suave and sophisticated young man by the time we started going out, a person who had it all together. I'm teasing, of course, but I would have hated to see what Michael was like if he hadn't been around young women before he met me. He certainly knew how to have fun and treat someone with honor.

I remember an incident that spoke volumes about Michael's character. We were in Waco, Texas, driving together down Interstate 35 to the Valley Mills Mall. Up ahead, on the freeway shoulder, a sedan was parked with the hood up. Smoke billowed from the engine in the summer heat.

Michael slowed down and pulled in behind the car, where a frazzled, middle-aged woman was wringing her hands. We stepped out, and Michael said, "I'm not much of a help under the hood, but I do have a cell phone. Shall I call for some roadside assistance?"

The woman was grateful, and after the automobile club had been summoned, we were back on our way. I have to tell you that I was greatly impressed that Michael would stop for a stranger and offer to help. That told me that he was someone special.

Some Fundamentals

Where do people get their knowledge about dating? As we suggested in chapter 1, the media offer lots of information that isn't very balanced. Some of you talk with each other about dating issues, and that can be good. Many of the people who attend our seminars ask us questions about dating, and we'd like to share some of the responses we give them. Whether this is new information or a refresher course for you, it doesn't hurt to review the dating fundamentals.

What's a good date?

To us, a good date is doing something that both people can enjoy together. If a guy is dragging his girlfriend to a ball game every Saturday night and she hates baseball, then that's a demonstration of who's more important in the relationship.

The Golden Rule is just as valid for a dating relationship. Your attitude should be, "What can I do that would be fun for her?" or "What can I do that would be fun for him?" This attitude demonstrates honor in the relationship.

How do personality types affect dates?

Personality types come into play when planning a date: a Steward guy may prefer to have a Captain girl plan something fun. If I (Michael) had tried to dominate the decision making that went into our dates, Amy wouldn't have gone for that. I'll never forget the time when Amy planned a "surprise date" that had us going to Lake Conroe outside of Houston for a day of riding jet skis. What an adrenaline rush! Remember, one of the qualities I was looking for was someone who was adventurous and not fearful. Whipping across Lake Conroe with Amy and making giant slalom turns on our jet skis certainly upped my admiration for her.

Amy even had a chance to play nursemaid for me that afternoon. I decided to impress her by getting some big air across some major wakes, but I hit one wrong and got launched into the air. Not knowing what I was doing, I kept my eyes open as we splashed into the lake, causing great eye pain. I thought I was going blind I was in so much pain. Amy came to the rescue with some tender loving care.

What about group dating?

Group dates, especially at the beginning of a dating rela-tionship, can be loads of fun and take the pressure off trying so hard to be witty, suave, urbane, and smooth-spoken. You can have a great time going to the county fair or out to dinner with another couple. Group dates also give you a window into how your date interacts with others.

Where's a good place to meet Christian guys and girls?

That's a tough one, especially after you leave college. Church and the Sunday school classes for young singles are obvious places to start. Also try attending Christian concerts, seminars, and other activities that put you in touch with Christian peers. You never know how God will orchestrate your meeting the right person. The point is, you increase your chances of meeting a Christian when you're in a place where Christians congregate. A Hooters bar on a Saturday night, for instance, might not have the largest dating pool of Christian bachelors and bachelorettes.

Is it safe to meet Christian dating partners on the Internet?

We are hearing from more and more Internet-savvy Christian singles who are connecting with that special person—or making reacquaintances—through the World Wide Web. Obviously, the world is a smaller place with Instant Messaging and e-mail. You can certainly keep in touch with an old flame from your hometown a lot more easily these days. The problem is that the contact on the Internet is not face-to-face, and there's nothing like interpersonal contact in a dating relationship.

On-line Christian personals and Christian dating services have gained in popularity, but be very, *very* careful. People can make up any persona they want on-line, and you can be sure that there are guys passing themselves off as women in chat rooms. If someone you meet on-line sounds like a soul mate, don't give out your address. Get to know that person on the phone first—preferably by using a cell-phone number.

Zany Date Ideas

What can you do on a date? Anything that allows you to get to know the other person. That's why going out to a restaurant is and always will be the prime-time dating experience. You share more than food over a dinner date; you share conversation.

Taking in a movie often ranks number two, but there's a built-in disadvantage when hitting the local Cineplex: You can't talk in a movie theater. Of course, you can chat up the film afterward at a coffeehouse or a dessert place, but that's not quite the same.

Since there's more than one way to make a date memorable, here are a few of our favorites:

Go out on a sports date. This one's a slam dunk, in our book. We just love doing outdoor things together. There's something about exercising in each other's company that does more than break a sweat. You break down communication barriers as well.

Sometimes you experience an unintended benefit from doing a sporting activity together. They say that sports don't build character—they reveal character. You can learn how your date handles adversity: What does he or she do when the windmill blocks the ball for the fourth time at the putt-putt golf course? Was the putter tossed into the parking lot? Did your date take out frustrations on the windmill? All kidding aside, you'll find other sports date opportunities out there:

- Riding mountain bikes on trails or through the foothills
- Taking a rock-climbing class together at a local indoor facility
- Skateboarding at a local skateboard park
- Taking part in a 10K run fund-raiser together
- Tossing a Frisbee around
- Joining a volleyball league

Enjoy a fast-food progressive date. Here's a fun group date that won't be forgotten soon. You and your buddies can drive to Taco Bell and buy some mucho grande three-cheese nachos. Then you can go to Mickey D's and split some salads. Then you can head off to your favorite fast-food chain (Carl's? Wendy's? BK? Subway?) for your entrée. Still hungry? You can top off your evening with dessert at a nice restaurant. (Did we hear anyone say the words *mud pie?*)

Play board games. There are a lot of great new board games out there these days: Malarky, Moods, Balderdash, Tri Bond, Cranium, and that old standby, Trivial Pursuit. Most need at least two or three couples to play, but you'll find the interaction great and the questions thought provoking—and revealing.

Play hide-and-seek with another couple at Wal-Mart. Now we're getting creative. Just as it's easy to get lost in Wal-Mart since the stores are so huge, it's also hard to find someone. Have fun dodging each other by moving from aisle to aisle.

Go on a scavenger hunt. Outfit each couple with a bag and a list of things to go hunting for: a can of tuna, a pair of red socks, a *TV Guide*, etc. Then go knocking on doors. Nonsense stuff is the best. You can all meet back at your place with your "take" and compare stories.

Have a homemade pizza night. Everyone knows that pizza is the all-American meal that draws from three of the major food groups. A Hawaiian Canadian Bacon pizza, for example, has meat (the Canadian bacon), bread (the crust), and fruit (the pineapple.) Buy all the ingredients at a grocery store: dough, pizza sauce, and toppings, and make the pizza back at your place. It helps to cook the pizza on a "pizza stone," but it's not absolutely necessary.

Create your own holiday. Go to the library, and put your hands on a book called *Chase's Annual Events*, which is filled with fun, off-the-wall holidays. You can invite your friends over for a party on holidays, such as French Fry Day on February 24; Peanut Butter Lover's Day on March 1; National Humor Month all during April; National Yo-Yo Day on June 6; and National Ice Cream Day on July 16.

Visit an animal shelter. Cats and dogs are so cute. It's fun to poke your fingers inside a few cages and say hello to some adorable pets. If you don't have the time to care for a dog, you could purchase a lonely pet together and give it to a child who would love to have it (and whose parents agree, of course).

Host a bubble mania. Who can make the largest bubble? Whose will fly the highest? Spend a few extra dollars and purchase huge bubble wands and a bigger supply of soap stuff. You'll go bonkers with the bubbles.

Go to a big football game together. Tailgating with friends on a crisp fall afternoon and later watching two football titans clash on the gridiron—life doesn't get better. (You can tell which one of us wrote that sentence.) Seriously, you can attend any sporting event that you would enjoy together, although, guys, you might not want to suggest beach volleyball, if you know what's good for you. Women's soccer might be a better bet. Baseball shouldn't be overlooked, either. Since nothing happens on the field most of the time, you have plenty of time to talk and discuss the weighty issues of the world.

Take in a show. There's something real about watching "live" actors and actresses make merry on the stage. It's just captivating, and the special effects can be stunning. The next time a nationwide tour of *Phantom of the Opera* or *Les Misérables* stops in your city, get tickets! Of course, a local revival of *Oklahoma!* or *Fiddler on the Roof* or *The Sound of Music* would be can't-miss bets, as well.

Dear Mike & Amy

I met this guy in the university choir, and I can tell he wants to go out with me. But I'm not feeling attracted to him at all because he seems a little pushy. How come he keeps sitting at my table for lunch?

—Protecting myself from a pushy guy

DEAR PROTECTING,

THERE'S A CHANCE THE GUY JUST WANTS TO GET TO KNOW YOU BETTER AND HE'S NOT SURE HOW TO START.

HOWEVER, IF YOUR INSTINCTS ARE RIGHT AND HE TRULY IS PUSHY, THEN HIS COMING TO YOUR TABLE MAY INDICATE THAT HE'S DESPERATE. AS WE ALL KNOW, GIVING OFF THOSE DESPERATION VIBES WILL KILL MORE BUDDING RELATIONSHIPS THAN BAD BREATH. WE CAN'T BLAME YOU FOR NOT FEELING ATTRACTED TO A GUY WHO TRAILS AFTER YOU LIKE A YORKSHIRE TERRIER; YOU CAN SENSE HIS PANIC EVERY TIME HE APPROACHES YOU.

SOME PEOPLE'S DESPERATION RISES FROM THEIR BELIEF THAT HAVING A BOYFRIEND OR A GIRLFRIEND WILL COM-

PLETE THEM, WHICH IS WHY THEY *TRY* SO HARD. THAT'S TOO BAD, BECAUSE PEOPLE WHO FEEL THEY HAVE TO BE DATING SOMEBODY TO BE HAPPY SABOTAGE THEIR OWN CHANCES EVERY TIME. DATING IN AND OF ITSELF WILL NEVER SATISFY A PERSON; ONLY A SOLID RELATIONSHIP IN JESUS CHRIST IS FULFILLING.

—Mike & Amy

Dear Mike & Amy,

At the office where I work, a guy has been showing some interest in me. He's cute, nice, a Christian, and in his early thirties. I'm twenty-two and just out of college. Is this too big of an age gap?

—Attracted to an older man

DEAR ATTRACTED,

I (MICHAEL) ONCE DATED A YOUNG WOMAN WHO WAS TWENTY-SEVEN. I WAS, AHEM, EIGHTEEN YEARS OLD, BUT KAREN THOUGHT I WAS TWENTY-ONE OR TWENTY-TWO. (I WAS SO MATURE FOR MY AGE. HA!) SHE SOON FOUND OUT THE REAL AGE DIFFERENCE, BUT THAT DIDN'T SEEM TO MATTER BECAUSE WE WERE SMITTEN WITH EACH OTHER.

AFTER SEVERAL MONTHS, HOWEVER, IT BECAME APPARENT TO ME THAT THIS WAS A RELATIONSHIP I DID NOT WANT TO CONTINUE FOR REASONS UNRELATED TO OUR AGE DIFFERENCE. BUT I DID LEARN SOME THINGS. KAREN WAS WAY AHEAD OF ME IN CERTAIN LIFE EXPERIENCES—COLLEGE, STARTING A CAREER, AND LIVING AND SUPPORTING HERSELF. THAT CERTAINLY CREATED SOME AWKWARD MOMENTS, AND I WONDERED MORE THAN A FEW TIMES IF I WAS "MATURE" ENOUGH FOR HER.

THE OTHER ISSUE RELATED TO MARRIAGE. AS WE'VE POINTED OUT BEFORE, MOST DATING RELATIONSHIPS DO NOT END IN MARRIAGE, BUT NEARLY ALL MARRIAGES START

WITH DATING. IF MY RELATIONSHIP WITH KAREN HAD AD-
VANCED AND IF OUR RELATIONSHIP HAD MOVED TOWARD
TAKING THE ULTIMATE STEP, THEN WHAT WOULD MARRIAGE
HAVE LOOKED LIKE BETWEEN US? WELL, WHEN I WOULD
HAVE BEEN TWENTY-ONE OR SO, SHE WOULD HAVE ROUNDED
THE CORNER ON THE AGE OF THIRTY. TALK ABOUT A
MAY–DECEMBER ROMANCE. THAT WOULD BRING SOME INTER-
ESTING DYNAMICS TO A MARRIAGE.

I'VE BEEN TALKING ABOUT THE AGE SITUATION IN RE-
LATION TO A YOUNGER MALE AND AN OLDER FEMALE.
WHAT'S MORE COMMON, OF COURSE, IS WHEN THE MALE IS
OLDER THAN THE FEMALE. AGAIN, OUR DESIRE IS TO NOT
SPELL OUT A CERTAIN AGE DIFFERENCE, BUT WITH OUR
COUNSELING BACKGROUND, WE MUST POINT OUT THAT MAR-
ITAL DIFFICULTIES MAY BE EXACERBATED BY A BROAD AGE
GAP BETWEEN THE PARTNERS—SOMETHING BEYOND TEN
YEARS.

LISTEN, I MARRIED SOMEONE OLDER: AMY HAS AN
ELEVEN-MONTH HEAD START ON ME. BUT AS THEY SAY IN
GOVERNMENT WORK, THAT'S CLOSE ENOUGH. IF YOU DO
DATE AND FALL IN LOVE WITH SOMEONE CONSIDERABLY
OLDER (OR YOUNGER), MAKE SURE YOU DISCUSS ALL THE
RAMIFICATIONS IN A PREMARITAL COUNSELING SITUA-
TION. IT'S BEST TO DEAL WITH THAT STUFF ON THE
FRONT END INSTEAD OF HAVING IT COME BACK TO HAUNT
YOU YEARS DOWN THE ROAD.

—Mike

Dear Mike & Amy,

This guy keeps asking me out, and I'm tempted to
say yes just to get him out of my hair. Am I going about this the right way?

—Tempted

NOT AT ALL. THE TRUTH IS ALWAYS THE BEST WAY TO HANDLE THINGS. AT THE END OF THE DAY, "PITY DATES" DON'T DO EITHER SIDE ANY GOOD, SO CONTINUE TO SAY NO WITH A SMILE. SOONER OR LATER HE'LL GET THE MESSAGE AND TURN HIS ATTENTIONS ELSEWHERE.

JUST A WARNING: IF THE GUY PERSISTS AND STARTS TO GET OBNOXIOUS, YOU'LL HAVE TO BE ASSERTIVE. GUYS WHO WON'T TAKE NO FOR AN ANSWER—THE TYPES WHO SEND FLOWERS EVERY OTHER DAY AND BOMBARD YOUR IN BOX WITH MESSAGES AND REQUESTS TO GO OUT—ARE DEMONSTRATING A NEEDY AND CONTROLLING PERSONALITY. AT A TIME WHEN WE'RE READING FAR TOO MANY NEWS REPORTS ABOUT STALKERS, IT WOULD BE SMART TO SAY THAT YOU WOULD APPRECIATE NEVER HEARING FROM HIM AGAIN.

—Mike & Amy

5
sex and the city

Shortly after Amy and I got married, and while I finished my senior year at Baylor University, I happened to be walking to chapel with Brett, a fraternity brother and a good guy. Brett was still single, as most college sophomores are.

"How is it being married?" he asked with a wicked grin. I knew exactly what he was talking about, so I gave him both barrels.

"Oh, let me tell you, being married is *great*," I said with the enthusiasm of someone still on his honeymoon. "I had sex this morning, and I can walk into chapel with a clear conscience."

"No way!"

"You'd better believe it."

I wasn't kidding my friend, and I won't kid you. Sex is great. That's exactly how Amy and I feel. Sex is better than great—it's awesome. We *love* making love, and we can say that without blushing. The one thing we're not going to do in *Don't Date Naked* is blow smoke and pretend otherwise.

But—and this is a very important *but* when it comes to sex—Amy and I are married. And because we're married, we can engage in one of life's greatest pleasures without feeling one tinge of guilt tugging at our souls.

Now that we have that point well taken care of, we're going to dive into a universally appealing subject that has fascinated artists, poets, authors, and filmmakers for centuries. Sex *is* interesting, and we wouldn't blame you if you have skipped ahead to this chapter before reading the others. We understand because it wasn't that long ago that we were young and single and couldn't wait to mingle. This is a very important chapter because sex and dating are intertwined: the former is never very far from the latter in the minds of daters. Sex is always *out there* because:

- You're still single, but you are also sexually mature, which means your hormones are working overtime, excreting all sorts of testosterone (for guys and, to a lesser extent, for females as well) that's causing your sexual appetite to balloon up like the appetite of a sumo wrestler who's missed his last two meals.

- You're hearing about sex morning, noon, and late into the night. It's impossible to escape the cultural "white noise" that bombards us with sex, sex, *sex*—24/7. Sex seeps out from every media outlet. Sex is constantly depicted, dissected, discussed, analyzed, and rhapsodized about in movies, videos, TV shows, music, magazines, advertisements, talk radio, and Web pages. Have I left anything out?

I'm sure I have, but stick with me here.

From our experience, many dating couples are having sex because our sex-saturated media *expect* them to have sex. As we mentioned earlier, the popular culture says that guys and girls who meet at a crosswalk are one date away from getting it on. With sex openly discussed in the classroom, just a click away on the Internet, and joked about on our entertainment shows, it's easy to have sex on the brain.

You'd think that everyone is having sex today since everyone is so hot and bothered about it, but that's not the case. Not everyone is doing it, and the percentage of teen boys and girls who have *not* had sex has actually increased in the last decade. "Choosing Virginity," a *Newsweek* cover story, reports that the Center for Disease Control indicates the percentage of high school students who have never had sexual intercourse rose by almost 10 percent between 1991 and 2001. That's a significant increase.[1]

Of course, that study is referring to young people eighteen and under, so you have to figure that a certain percentage of young adults are losing their virginity between the time they graduate from high school and the time they get married. Having said that, if you are still a virgin, you are a member of a minority group. In a different way, you're countercultural, and we salute you.

We know how tough it is to remain pure. Amy and I made it to our wedding night without having sex, but it was very tough. The sexual pressure we felt was *intense*.

There's no doubt that you're feeling that sexual intensity as well. There's also no doubt that Christian singles are having sex. We know because they *tell* us. (Don't forget that Amy and I meet with lots of people in our seminars and we host a youth group in our home every week.)

One night at a concert at church, I noticed everyone was getting crazy in the mosh pit as a Christian band named Mary's Eye played. In the midst of the chaos, Jason Brawner (another youth group leader) and I saw a boy—a Christian teen—palming a girl's breast, really groping her. After breaking it up, Jason took the boy aside and let him know in no uncertain terms that what he did was out of bounds. Later on that evening, I decided to take the boy and four other kids to McDonald's after the concert. We needed to talk because these kids were giving me flak because "the palmer" got disciplined.

As we chowed down on a late-night snack of Big Macs and supersized fries, I had a question for them. "Who gropes?" I asked.

(I use the word *groping* instead of *petting*, which sounds like something out of *Pleasantville*. I don't know about you, but whenever I hear the word *petting*, I think of petting a goat at the zoo. *Fondling* is another word I don't hear kids using these days.)

Four of the five raised their hands to acknowledge that they had groped in the past.

"Who's still a virgin?" I asked.

All their hands went down.

"There's your reason. That's why it's not a good idea to grope," I said.

I let that thought settle for a moment before hitting them with another question. "How many of you are still with that person you last had sex with?"

This time no one raised his or her hand.

Again, that's my point: When you have sex before marriage, ninety-nine times out of a hundred the relationship will crumble. You will end up destroying what you spent so long in building up. If you want your relationship to last, then the last thing you want to do is have sex. And if you do have sex, you have to be prepared to acquire one of the Big Three: the HIV virus (the precursor to AIDS), any number of other sexually transmitted diseases, or a six-pound "surprise" nine months later.

Let's talk about the HIV virus and AIDS first. Just because AZT and other anti-retroviral drug "cocktails" are making a long life possible for many infected with HIV, it doesn't mean that you're out of the woods. I have one word for you: Africa. The Dark Continent is being ravaged by the worst health calamity since the Middle Ages' bubonic plague. AIDS in Africa is being spread, for the most part, by heterosexual sex. And the HIV virus gets passed around like a party favor.

Here in the States young people seem to think that since Magic Johnson appears to be doing all right these days, then it's okay to go out and have sex—as long as you use a condom. That type of thinking remains misguided at best and patently stupid at worst. You still get AIDS from sleeping around.

Reality cannot be ignored: If you have sex with someone who is HIV-positive, you are playing Russian roulette with a pistol in which several of the barrels contain deadly bullets. How many? Hard to say, but even if there is only one, you are taking too great a risk. And all this blather about using a condom to "protect" yourself should be taken with a grain of salt. The HIV virus is far smaller than human sperm (the HIV virus is about .002 the size of the human sperm), so the virus can pass through the pores of a condom like water through a sieve.

If HIV weren't enough, we have a rat's nest of other sexually transmitted diseases to worry about. One in four—that's 25 percent for those of you keeping score at home—teens having sex will acquire an STD. More than twenty STDs have been identified, according to the National Institutes of Health, and it's an impressive roll call: chlamydia, herpes, genital warts, gonorrhea, and syphilis comprise the STD all-stars.

These STDs are incredibly easy to pick up if you're sleeping around with someone who's been sleeping around. Dr. C. Everett Koop, the former U.S. Surgeon General, once warned, "When you have sex with someone, you are having sex with everyone they have had sex with for the last ten years, and everyone their partners have had sex with the last ten years." That can add up to be a lot of people—and triple or quintuple your chances for being infected by an ugly STD. Dr. Kevin Leman, author of *Adolescence Isn't Terminal*, said the grossest thing he ever saw was the young client who pulled back her shorts a bit to reveal a string of unsightly sores running down the inside of her thighs.[2]

Condoms are also ineffective against preventing the spread of human papilloma virus (HPV), which causes 90 percent of Americans' cancers of the cervix, vagina, vulva, and penis.[3] Ken Connor, president of the Family Research Council, says this about condom use against STDs: "Telling young people they can engage in sexual conduct and avoid STDs by using condoms is like throwing someone a life preserver in a tidal wave."[4]

Then there are the other unintended consequences of premarital sexual activity: children. When a young unmarried woman becomes pregnant, she's really opening Pandora's box. Too many young women have gone to the abortion table and lived with a lifetime of regret. If the young woman carries her child to term, then what happens? Does she marry the guy and make the best of the situation—for the rest of her life? That's assuming the guy will agree to marry her. According to demographer Larry Bumpass, one-third of first-born children of unmarried women will spend their childhood without married parents.[5] Unwed childbearing leaves parents and children economically disadvantaged. Everyone pays a price: the mother, the father, and the child. And like ripples in a pond that splash up on a shoreline far away, the ramifications of unwed pregnancy can be felt for several generations.

So, it's best to wait. And the best reason to wait to have sex until you're married is because that's God's good plan. And we honor him when we follow his plan.

In his mercy God warns us in the Scriptures of the dangers of not waiting. Even I—who was a virgin on my wedding night and skipped to that oversized bed because I was so excited to make love for the first time—was deeply affected by my wife's decision to have sex with another guy before we got married.

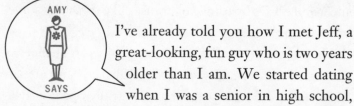

I've already told you how I met Jeff, a great-looking, fun guy who is two years older than I am. We started dating when I was a senior in high school, and our relationship kicked up a notch during the college years, even though the schools we attended were one hundred miles apart. For the first year or two, a hundred miles didn't seem very far. As we drew closer and closer, we both felt the urge to let ourselves go, but I stuck to my guns and did not give in sexually to him. Then the summer before my sophomore year at Baylor, Jeff broke up with me. He said that handling a long-distance relationship during a very difficult senior year of college would be too much for him. Jeff couldn't see himself juggling a girl-friend and his studies at the same time.

The news devastated me. I was absolutely heartbroken and thought my world had come to an end. The breakup crushed me like nothing else. We remained "good friends," however. Over the next few months, I would hear from Jeff occasionally when he called to see how I was doing. One time he asked if I was dating anyone. That question felt like a dagger in my heart. I was so hurt that I said we could not be friends any longer.

"You are being so silly," he said. "We can still be friends."

"Jeff, I can't. This is too painful for me."

I went off on a crying jag for twenty-four hours until I realized that the sun would rise the following morning. I decided to put Jeff behind me and get a life. I began going out with anybody who asked me for a date, but each time I sat next to some guy in a darkened movie theater, I remembered the tremendous amount of rejection I felt from Jeff.

Thinking about my ex-boyfriend all the time drove me crazy. When the school year ended and I went home to Houston for the summer, I decided that I could not go on like this. I couldn't put Jeff behind me. He was the person I was in love with, I decided. I wanted him to be my husband and live happily ever after.

I hatched a plan to win him back. I was going to make him love me. What would be the thing that would make him fall in love with me all over again? It would be proving my love by going to bed with him.

One midsummer weekend, I drove to Dallas to attend a cheerleading camp. I knew Jeff was in Dallas working as an intern. I had seen him the weekend before when he dropped by my home. We tossed around a Frisbee and talked a little bit. I sensed the door opening just a crack. When I casually mentioned that I was going to be in Dallas the following weekend, he said, "Yeah, maybe we can get together."

I wanted this rejection to end. If I took the penultimate step in our relationship and did have sex with him, then he would see what he was missing. When I arrived in Dallas that fateful Friday night, I was supposed to stay at a girl-friend's house, but I called Jeff and told him I needed a place to stay.

"Would it be okay if I stayed at your apartment?" I asked.

"Sure," he said, probably thinking that I would sleep on his living room couch. "I'm sure my roommate won't mind. His girlfriend is coming over. Would you mind if we go out together with them?"

Double date, single date . . . it didn't matter to me. Later that evening when we were at a restaurant, I sent out clear signals that I wanted to pick up our relationship where it left off.

When Jeff and I got back to his apartment, a third buddy was there, and they decided to go swimming in the apartment pool. I stayed in Jeff's bedroom while they had their fun. Fifteen minutes later Jeff knocked on the door and walked in. He was wearing a towel and had a huge grin across his face.

He sat down next to me on his bed. We didn't say a word. He kissed me, and within a few minutes, the deed was done. I had given Jeff my prized possession—my virginity—in a last-ditch attempt to win back his love.

You probably can figure out the rest of the story: Becoming sexually active together was the beginning of the end of our relationship. Sure, there was a "warming period" in our relationship, and we eventually became engaged. I really thought Jeff would love me and treat me differently after I continually gave myself to him, but that didn't happen. The old adage—*women give sex to get love and men give love to get sex*—was certainly true in my case. Instead of rekindling our love for each other, my decision to become physical with him mortally wounded our relationship. I thought making love would secure his love; instead, it made me feel extremely insecure because now I had given him everything I had—and it was turning out not to be enough. What more could I do? The ball was totally in his court, and I had no leverage at all.

My decision to have sex with Jeff tripped the law of unintended consequences. I knew I was changing the course of my life that evening, but I had no idea of the far-reaching consequences that I would face. Not only did our relationship disintegrate, but I felt disappointed with myself. I also knew I had disappointed God. I felt guilt because I knew my actions were not what God wanted for me. In the back of my mind I knew what the Bible said about waiting for sex until marriage, but I chose to ignore God's wisdom. When I came to my senses, I had to admit that God sets boundaries on our physical relationships because he loves us, not because he doesn't want us to enjoy good things.

I'm so grateful that I did not develop STDs as a result of my sexual involvement. I know people who didn't escape, and it's not a pretty sight.

Then there are the consequences in our marriage. These really surprised me. My marital life with Michael became extremely difficult during our first year of marriage, and I'm not exaggerating when I say that our marriage barely survived the turmoil. Michael worried constantly about how he measured up as a lover compared to Jeff. He was a virgin when we married, and he told me that he wondered what I was thinking during our most intimate moments—if what he was doing was right or better or worse than something Jeff had done. Those feelings of inadequacy hurt Michael deeply, and it was all because I had given myself to Jeff. I had disappointed myself and disappointed God, and my marriage became a private hell.

MICHAEL SAYS

I haven't forgotten how frustrated, unsure, anxious, and worried I was about the future of my marriage, and it took Amy and me eighteen months to turn a corner. We needed counseling to work through some heavy-duty issues.

You see, I had grown up knowing how important it was to save myself for marriage. My parents reminded me until they were blue in the face that the Bible says that we are not to have sex unless we are married. Perhaps you've had those same lessons drummed into your head as well. But my parents were right. Scripture is quite clear about how God has reserved sex for marriage.

Before you read the following verses, it's important to know the meaning behind some of the words. In several of the older versions of the Bible, the English word *fornication* was used to refer to sex outside of marriage. *Fornication* is translated from the Greek word *porneia*, which shares a root with our word *pornography*. Many modern translations merely translate the Greek word as "sexual immorality" or "sexual sin." We've italicized the words that refer to sex before marriage.

> Run away from sexual sin! No other sin so clearly affects the body as this one does. For *sexual immorality* is a sin against your own body. *(1 Corinthians 6:18)*

> And that means killing off everything connected with that way of death: *sexual promiscuity*, impurity, lust, doing whatever you feel like whenever you feel like it, and grabbing whatever attracts your fancy. That's a life shaped by things and feelings instead of by God. *(Colossians 3:5, THE MESSAGE)*

> God wants you to be holy, so you should keep clear of all *sexual sin*. Then each of you will control your body and live in holiness and honor—not in lustful passion as the pagans do, in their ignorance of God and his ways. *(1 Thessalonians 4:3-5)*

Let there be no *sexual immorality,* impurity, or greed among you. Such sins have no place among God's people. *(Ephesians 5:3)*

So put to death the sinful, earthly things lurking within you. Have nothing to do with *sexual sin,* impurity, lust, and shameful desires. Don't be greedy for the good things of this life, for that is idolatry. *(Colossians 3:5)*

What I meant was that you are not to keep company with anyone who claims to be a brother Christian but indulges in *sexual sins.* . . . Don't even eat lunch with such a person. *(1 Corinthians 5:11, TLB)*

With those reminders from God's Word ringing in your ears, how can you pace yourself so that you remain sexually pure? Remember: Don't date naked. Put on the clothing that will guarantee you success in dating. Here are some tips:

Commit to Purity

The paraphrase of Ephesians 6 inserted into the introduction to this book says, "In every dating situation you will need a commitment to purity as your shield to stop the fiery arrows of temptation aimed at you by Satan." The first important step is to make a conscious decision to remain pure. Purity doesn't "just happen." It's the result of a decision and a commitment.

What we *can* guarantee will "just happen" is temptation. You know this from your own experience. Our enemy, Satan, has lots of tricks and strategies to trip us up, and he knows how powerful sexual temptation is.

A shield protects. Protect your heart, emotions, and body with the shield of purity. That means purity not only in your actions but also in your mind and heart. Stay away from anything that will get your sexual juices flowing. Guys, don't think that you can look at pornography and keep your minds pure. Put a lock on it.

This next statement may be so obvious that it may not need to be said: Make sure the person you date has the same commitment to purity. If he or she doesn't, you will be fighting an uphill battle.

Set Your Limits Early

Once you have taken up the shield of purity, communicate your decision. Set your limits early. You might want to set limits on the first date to dampen any expectations later that evening. When you make a stand early, you usually never have to make a stand again. We heard about one girl who told her date, "In case you're wondering, I have drawn my limit at my neck, so if you have any plans for dating me for any period of time, you better pace yourself." I dated several young women who set their limits early with me. Because they did this, I respected them, and I never, ever pressured them to become sexually involved.

Set those limits, and stick to them. Stack the odds in your favor by not going into each other's apartments for a late-night cup of coffee or by not watching a video at your place when your roommates are gone. You need account-ability. It's those little things that keep you from doing *big* things.

Set Your Limits Wisely

How far is too far? We think you should stop at first base—kissing. Sure, you may want to round first base a bit and French kiss some, but even that can lead you out of bounds and should be kept to a minimum. Once you start French kissing, your hands want to go places normally covered by bathing suit tops and bottoms, and once your hands go there, you're groping. Once you're groping, oral sex is just a zipper pull away.

If kissing is your limit—as it should be—you might think about taking a "holiday" from kissing every now and then so that smooching still feels special. Remember, sex is progressive and always wants to rush forward at the speed of light.

Some Christian books frustrate me because they don't want to tell you what's too far. I would say that a great line to draw is that if you can't do it in front of your parents or in a public venue with adults you respect, then you shouldn't be doing what you're doing.

Honor Yourself and Your Dating Partner

While staying sexually pure is first of all a matter of fol-lowing God's good plan for relationship, it is also a matter of honor. Obviously, you honor God when you follow his instructions. But you also need to honor yourself and your dating partner.

What does that mean? You are a person of honor when you do the right thing, when you treat the other person with deep respect and care. The New Testament tells us to "love each other with genuine affection, and take delight in honoring each other" (Romans 12:10).

Do you honor the person you are dating? Do you look out for his or her needs before your own? Are you self-centered? Are you considerate? Do you ask him or her to do things that are potentially harmful? Do you respect his or her limits?

When you date, clothe yourself with honor. As one of the previously quoted Bible verses reminds you, "God wants you to be holy, so you should keep clear of all sexual sin. Then each of you will control your body and live in holiness and honor" (1 Thessalonians 4:3-4).

Establish Accountability Relationships

One of the most important ways you can help a dating relationship is to establish accountability relationships with people who will help you stick to your goals. Again, don't date naked. Put on the belt of accountability.

If it's hard for you to admit that you need help, let us say as loudly as we can: *You're going to need help!* Remember what we've said before. So much of our culture encourages and expects premarital sexual involvement. In fact, our culture often makes fun of people who are not sexually active. You'll need help in combating the cultural pressure.

What do accountability relationships look like? They can be as simple as asking a close friend to check up on you often, asking how you are doing in your commitment to purity in your dating relationship, in what you see in movies, in what sites you visit on the Web. Again, this may go without saying, but ask only those friends who would value sexual purity as much as you do.

Or, accountability can take the form of a group. We know of college students who have formed small groups who meet to check up on each other, encourage each other, and pray for each other. Amy and I have formed small groups within the youth group we help to lead, and some of those groups focus on accountability in dating relationships as well as accountability in a person's spiritual life.

Some people have accountability relationships with parents, who have given them purity rings and have pledged to pray for their son or daughter to remain chaste. Those are important accountability relationships, but we recommend that once you move out of the house to take a job or go to school, establish accountability beyond your family. We know young people who have asked an older couple whom they respect to be their accountability partners.

Sexual temptation is so strong and accountability so important that we know married Christian men who have placed themselves in regular accountability relationships because they know their marriages depend on it. One group of men who regularly travel call themselves "The Order of the Towel." When one of them is on the road and in a hotel, the others call to ask a question: "Where is your towel?" The agreement is that they will put a towel over the TV to remind them of their commitment not to watch anything remotely pornographic.

One more thought. We have found that accountability works best if it goes both ways. What we mean by that is that you are more likely to have a healthy dating relationship if you are helping others to have pure, healthy dating relationships.

Think Long-term

So many couples get caught up in the sexual excitement, and before they know it, clothes are flying everywhere. It's so hard to back up on the freeway of sex. When you are tempted to go too far physically, think about your wedding night. Don't you want that evening—and early morning—to be one of those once-in-a-lifetime moments? Waiting will make your wedding night the most wonderful and guilt-free experience. It was for me, although it wasn't quite the same for Amy. (My issues with Jeff cropped up during the honeymoon, and things got so bad that we cut our Caribbean cruise honeymoon short and flew back to the States.)

Know Your Own Limits

If you're a male virgin and your dating partner wants to have sex, watch out. I was once mentoring a college guy who had never dated before. Then he found a girlfriend, and he was all excited for his future. One evening I asked Chris, "How are you doing physically?"

"Oh, we're doing okay," he said.

"Well, what does that mean?" I followed up. "Are you having sex?" You can tell I don't like to beat around the bush when it comes to these matters.

"No. She kind of wants to, but I don't want to."

I cautioned him to remain strong. "If you think you can resist, you won't make it. There is not a guy on earth strong enough to resist if the girl actually wants to do it," I said. I also warned that since Samson and Delilah guys have fallen to women beckoning them to bed.

Several months later, Chris was a mess and needed to talk. Through tears, he told me that his girlfriend created scenarios where it would be easy for them to have sex—her roommate was gone for the weekend, for instance—yet he held out and continued to resist her enticements for two months. Then he fell like a tall fir dropped in the forest.

"Had you broken off the relationship with her, this wouldn't have happened," I said, stating the obvious. "I think you need to end the relationship now because she is not the person you want to date."

So mark my words, guys. If she comes on to you, don't

be flattered. Be thinking about saying good-bye and dating someone else.

Keep Your Clothes On

We've used the phrase *don't date naked* in the figurative sense in this book, but here we mean it literally. Keep your clothes on and your zippers zipped. We said earlier that once you start groping, oral sex is just a zipper pull away. We're serious.

We know how casually young people treat oral sex these days. Ever since the Lewinsky–Clinton scandal, oral sex left the pages of the *Penthouse Forum* and leaped onto the front pages of our daily newspapers. Everyone started talking about oral sex, and kids were listening. The former White House intern said she and the president weren't having sex; they were just "fooling around." And President Clinton argued their sexual encounter did not rise to the legal definition of what sex is.

As ABC's John Stossel would say, "Give me a break," but many young couples don't see it that way. When I do premarital counseling with couples, I like to know what I'm getting into, so I always probe into their sexual history. That can be significant, because if one or both have been sexually active, there's usually guilt involved, and that's something you definitely want to deal with in premarital counseling.

I remember the time I was counseling Rick and Rhonda.

"You don't have to answer any of these questions," I began, "but it would help me if I can ask you several questions about your sexual past. Would that be okay?"

They both nodded, so I proceeded. "Have either of you ever had sex?" I asked.

They both turned to each other and shrugged.

"No, I haven't," Rick stated.

"Me either," said Rhonda.

"Very good. Have either of you had oral sex?"

Without batting an eye, they both said, "Sure."

When I prompted them for more information, their attitude was, "It's no big deal. At least we're not having sex."

To many young people, casual oral sex is like making out. Our stance, however, is that oral sex is sex and therefore not appropriate outside of marriage. Remember what Ephesians 5:3 says? "Let there be no sexual immorality, impurity, or greed among you. Such sins have no place among God's people."

That's why we feel anything beyond kissing is too far. If that sounds fuddy-duddy to you, then ask people who've gone too far if they had oral sex. I will guarantee you that nearly all of them have.

If you were at one of our seminars, Amy and I might take some time here to have some straight talk about setting limits. So, allow us to do that now. We both have some things to say—Amy from a female perspective, and I from a male perspective. Because males and females are different in some significant ways, we want to talk to you separately. But we encourage females to listen in to what we say to guys, and vice versa. We think you'll learn a few things.

MICHAEL & AMY'S STRAIGHT TALK ABOUT SETTING LIMITS

MICHAEL TALKS TO GUYS

1. Check your motives for why you are dating. Is it to have a healthy friendship with a girl? Is it to satisfy your physical desires?

2. Don't place all of the responsibility of setting boundaries on the girl.

3. If you respect the girl and want the relationship to last, ask her where her boundaries are. And don't forget to set your own boundaries by the yardstick we mentioned earlier in the Scripture verses.

AMY TALKS TO GUYS

1. Remember that most girls enter a relationship for close friendship, not for a hot physical relationship.

2. Most girls want you to respect them without needing to remind you.

3. This may not be an easy conversation for you—or for her. But make it safe. Say something like, "I want you to know you are more important than anything physical that happens between us. I want us to feel good about every part of this relationship. Can we talk about where we're going to set our limits?" We emphasize the *we* because it's important not to make her feel like the bad guy.

4. Give her permission to stop you—and then *stop* if she asks you to. You honor her when you respect her feelings.

4. Don't use this as an excuse to push, but let her know that she has the right to stop you. Say something like, "Anytime you feel uncomfortable, even if it's just kissing me, will you let me know?" Asking questions allows her to open up and tell you how she feels.

5. You don't have to be a Casanova on a date. And you don't have to report to your buddies the next morning. Keeping the relationship physically safe is just between you and your dating partner.

5. Don't kiss and tell. There is nothing that can destroy trust more than your going into detail about what the two of you have and have not done. If you brag to your friends, she'll be smart to break up with you when she finds out. A girl's reputation is precious, so don't ruin it for her!

6. Purity in your relationship is all about planning. Don't rely on your will—it WILL fail you.

6. You need to be just as proactive about purity as your girlfriend. Don't rely on her to be your conscience.

7. Long make-out sessions are off-limits. Being alone in a bedroom is off-limits. Staying the night is off-limits. Don't set yourself up to fail.

7. I add a few more suggestions: Double-date as often as possible; there is strength in numbers. If it's late, don't start the movie.

MICHAEL TALKS TO GIRLS

1. How a guy sets limits and respects your limits says a lot about him. If he doesn't respect your physical limits, how do you expect him to respect you in other areas?

2. If the guy seems to be pushing beyond where you'd like to go, say, "Stop. I'm not comfortable with this."

3. Just because you might be able to stop after kissing for long periods of time doesn't mean your boyfriend can do the same. It's not fair to push him farther than he can handle. Don't lead a guy on physically, please, for his sake!

4. If you commit yourself to purity, you need to live out your decision through a support group of girls who meet every week to ask you the tough question, "How are you doing sexually?"

AMY TALKS TO GIRLS

1. It would be ideal if the guy had the same limits you do, but if he doesn't take the initiative to set them, then you can—and should. Say something like, "I'm not comfortable with heavy kissing, so please don't push me."

2. Do your part to help the guy stay in line. Remember how a guy is wired. If you get stuck in a situation, tell him, "I hear my conscience calling." Make him laugh, and then get out of the situation.

3. If you light the fire, expect to get burned. Females can shut it off a lot faster than males can. You are wrong if you lead him down a path you know you're not ready to go down.

4. It's difficult to find people who want to talk about remaining pure. Find a Bible study—or start one—that can provide accountability as well as spiritual growth.

5. Don't put yourself into compromising positions or places that you will regret afterward.

6. If you're angry with your dad, work on forgiving him. Often a female's anger with her father leads to promiscuity.

7. Don't look for approval in the arms of a boy. Find it in the grasp of your heavenly Father.

8. Boys will never make you happy!

9. Be strong, and know your value before you get into a dating relationship. If you do, your chances of remaining pure are greatly increased.

5. I agree. Just don't go there.

6. Be aware that when females seek affection from men, they often are looking for affection that is missing from their relationship with their fathers.

7. Remember, you can't make a guy love you by having sex with him.

8. I agree. We women know it, but it's hard to live it. Find happiness in your relationship to God.

9. You are priceless. Remember that Jesus died for you. You are worth the best. Don't settle for anything less.

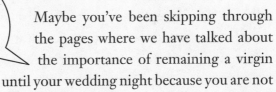

Maybe you've been skipping through the pages where we have talked about the importance of remaining a virgin until your wedding night because you are not a virgin. Perhaps it's too painful to contemplate that you will never be able to say to your future spouse, "I saved myself for you."

I can feel your pain, and it hurts to this day because it's something I couldn't say to Michael either. As much as I wanted to roll back the clock and undo what I did with Jeff, I can't do that. I had sex before I married Michael. If you're in the same boat, if you've already been sexually active, you need to do two things that I did:

1. *Repent of your sin and ask God to forgive you.* Once you confess your sin and admit your need for God's forgiveness, he will forgive you and blot out your sin. The Lord tells us in Isaiah 43:25 that "I—yes, I alone—am the one who blots out your sins for my own sake and will never think of them again." Notice what this passage says: "I will never think of them again." God's forgiveness is complete. He doesn't see me and say, "That's the person who had sex before she was married." Because of the death and resurrection of Jesus, God looks at me and says, "I accept my Son's sacrifice for your sin. You are clean." Think of it. Clean. That doesn't mean that I haven't felt the consequences of my sin, but I am no longer guilty. I've confessed my sin and repented—turned away from the sin.

If you haven't repented, please do so today! The rest of your life is ahead of you, and it's worth it to obey God's direction to reserve sex for marriage. He created this boundary for our protection: to protect us from a host of sexually transmitted diseases; to protect us from the possibility of becoming a parent before we are mature enough or financially able to support and raise that child; and to protect our minds from making sexual comparisons when we marry.

2. *Commit yourself to remain pure until your wedding day.* Part of repenting—going in a different direction—is committing yourself to remain pure, as we mentioned earlier in this chapter. This could be difficult, especially if you are still having a relationship with the person you had sex with. If you accept God's forgiveness, repent and turn away, commit yourself to sexual purity, and have others to hold you accountable, you can remain pure. It will be like starting fresh, with a clean slate.

After I broke up with Jeff, I repented for what I had done and promised God that I would not have sex until my marriage night. I kept that vow, although as Michael said, it was not easy. But it was our commitment to that goal—not to engage in sexual intercourse prior to marriage—that kept us from going any further. We set boundaries, and those boundaries saved us in the end.

don't date naked

Dear Mike & Amy,

My boyfriend and I just had sex for the first time. We didn't plan on doing it; it just happened. Now what do we do?

—Scared and confused

Dear Scared and Confused,

We are so sorry you and your boyfriend took such a major step in your relationship. Your feelings of confusion and fear are normal responses to having premarital sex. This is why God wants us to save sex for marriage—a dating relationship doesn't have the capacity to withstand the intimacy sex brings to a relationship.

Consequently, most sexually active dating relationships end in a breakup. We aren't telling you to end the relationship, but you may need to. We are saying it is going to be extremely hard to keep it together. The two of you have crossed a boundary not meant to be crossed, and there will be consequences for it.

If you do stay together, you'll have to set up very serious boundaries on your physical relationship or you will continue having sex. It is so hard to stop sex in a dating relationship once it begins.

A very important part of the decision about whether the two of you should stay together is how your boyfriend feels. If he's not upset or sorry about what happened, then you will need to end the relationship. Both of you need to be recommitted to purity, or it won't work. If he's as upset as you seem to be, then you need to have a very serious talk and set up some safeguards so that it won't "just happen" again.

Our recommendation would be to eliminate alone

99

TIME IN PRIVATE ROOMS, CARS, OR WHEREVER YOU COULD GET INTO TROUBLE PHYSICALLY. THEN YOU NEED TO GET INTO ACCOUNTABILITY RELATIONSHIPS, LIKE THE ONES WE'VE DISCUSSED IN THIS CHAPTER, TO MAKE SURE YOU HAVE STRONG FRIENDS HELPING THE TWO OF YOU KEEP YOUR COMMITMENT OF NOT HAVING SEX AGAIN.

OUR GUESS IS THAT YOU ARE PROBABLY ALSO FEELING GUILTY ABOUT WHAT YOU HAVE DONE. THAT'S NATURAL. WHEN WE BREAK ONE OF GOD'S GOOD BOUNDARIES FOR US, WE FEEL THE GUILT. GUILT IS A LIKE A WARNING LIGHT THAT TELLS US SOMETHING IS WRONG. THE GOOD NEWS IS THAT WHEN WE CONFESS OUR SIN TO GOD, HE IS FAITHFUL TO FORGIVE US. DON'T IGNORE THE WARNING LIGHT. CONFESS YOUR BEHAVIOR TO GOD, AND ASK—AND RE-CEIVE—HIS FORGIVENESS. YOU MIGHT WANT TO TALK WITH A SPIRITUALLY MATURE PERSON—A PASTOR OR LEADER AT CHURCH, AN OLDER FRIEND—WHO CAN HELP YOU FIND THAT FORGIVENESS.

—Mike & Amy

Dear Mike & Amy,

I've had sex before with a couple of girls. Does it even matter for me to stop now?

—Already did it

DEAR ALREADY DID IT,

YES! YES! YES! IT TRULY MATTERS TO STOP NOW. TOO MANY YOUNG PEOPLE HAVE SEX BEFORE MARRIAGE AND JUST SAY, "OH WELL, TOO LATE NOW. I'M NOT A VIRGIN AND CAN NEVER BE ONE AGAIN, SO I'LL JUST KEEP HAVING SEX."

THIS IS A FAULTY THOUGHT PROCESS. WE ONCE READ IN A BOOK THAT SIN IS LIKE AN OBNOXIOUS YAPPING DOG ON THE OUTSIDE OF A DOOR. WE MAY LET THIS STUPID LIT-TLE DOG IN BECAUSE IT SAYS THINGS LIKE, "DON'T

WORRY, I WON'T BITE. IT'S NO BIG DEAL. I'M NOT GO-
ING TO HURT ANYONE. I JUST WANT TO COME INSIDE."

THEN WE OPEN THE DOOR, AND THE LITTLE DOG LEAPS AT
OUR LEGS AND STARTS BITING. MANY CHRISTIANS REAL-
IZE THE MISTAKE OF LETTING THIS YAPPING DOG INSIDE
OF THEIR HOUSES, BUT THEN THEY DON'T KNOW WHAT TO
DO. THEY TRY TO TAME THE DOG. WHEN THAT DOESN'T
WORK, THEY KICK THEMSELVES FOR LETTING THE DOG IN.
INSTEAD OF KICKING THEMSELVES, THEY NEED TO BE
KICKING OUT THE DOG THAT'S BITING THEIR LEG.

THE SAME IS TRUE FOR YOU. PUT THE DOG OUT THE
DOOR. PUT AWAY THE SIN. STOP HAVING SEX. DON'T LET
YOUR PAST DICTATE YOUR FUTURE. YOU CAN STOP AND BE-
COME RENEWED AGAIN THROUGH CHRIST, WHO STRENGTHENS
US!

—Mike & Amy

Dear Mike & Amy,

I always hear that I'm not allowed to have "sexual intercourse." So I don't. But my girlfriend
and I do have oral sex and enjoy groping each
other. Is that a problem?

—Haven't gone all the way

DEAR HAVEN'T GONE ALL THE WAY,

YOU MAY NOT HAVE GONE "ALL THE WAY," BUT YOU'VE AL-
READY GONE WAY TOO FAR. YES! HAVING ORAL SEX AND
GROPING EACH OTHER ARE BIG PROBLEMS. DESPITE WHAT
YOU MAY HAVE BEEN TOLD, ORAL SEX IS SEX. A BURGLAR
IS A THIEF WHETHER HE STEALS $100 OR $100,000.

ORAL SEX AND PLAYING AROUND WITH EACH OTHER'S
BODIES ARE JUST AS DAMAGING AND DANGEROUS AS HAVING
ACTUAL INTERCOURSE. WE WANT TO BE CLEAR: WHEN IT
COMES TO ORAL SEX AND GROPING, DON'T GO THERE.

NOW YOU HAVE A PROBLEM. WHAT ARE YOU GOING TO DO

ABOUT THE FACT THAT YOU'VE GONE TOO FAR? RATCHETING
BACK FROM ORAL SEX WILL BE A TOUGH JOB. DON'T THINK
THAT YOU CAN DO IT ALONE.

FIRST, PRAY ABOUT IT. WE'RE SERIOUS. WE WANT YOU
TO PRAY ABOUT HAVING HAD ORAL SEX. CONFESS NOT ONLY
THAT WHAT YOU DID WAS WRONG BUT ALSO THAT YOU CAN'T
RESIST ON YOUR OWN POWER. THEN CLOTHE YOUR DATING
RELATIONSHIP IN PRAYER. REMEMBER THE PARAPHRASE OF
EPHESIANS 6 THAT WE MADE IN THE INTRODUCTION TO
THIS BOOK?

> *BE STRONG WITH THE LORD'S MIGHTY POWER.
> DON'T DATE NAKED. CLOTHE YOURSELF WITH ALL
> OF THE PROTECTION GOD HAS PROVIDED SO THAT
> YOU WILL BE ABLE TO STAND FIRM AGAINST ALL
> STRATEGIES AND TRICKS OF THE DEVIL. FOR WHEN
> YOU DATE, YOU WILL FACE TEMPTATIONS AND
> CHALLENGES THAT ARE BEYOND YOUR ABILITY TO
> FIGHT ALONE. YOU WILL NEED GOD'S GRACE,
> LOVE, WISDOM, AND POWER. YOU WILL NEED HELP
> FROM FRIENDS WHO ARE COMMITTED TO YOUR GOOD.
> YOU WILL NEED A SPECIAL WARDROBE FOR THE
> CHALLENGE.*
>
> *SO GET DRESSED. PUT ON ALL OF THE CLOTHING
> GOD HAS PROVIDED SO THAT YOU WILL STAND
> FIRM. STAND YOUR GROUND, PUTTING ON THE ROBE
> OF PRAYER, WHICH WILL COVER YOU, SUBMITTING
> YOURSELF AND YOUR FUTURE TO GOD'S PLAN.*

RECOMMITTING YOURSELF TO PURITY ONCE YOU HAVE EN-
GAGED IN SEX MAY BE ONE OF THE HARDEST THINGS YOU
DO. AND YOU CAN BE SURE THAT THE DEVIL WILL TRY VERY
HARD TO LURE YOU WITH HIS STRATEGIES AND TRICKS.
STAND FIRM.

SECOND, MAKE SURE YOU AND YOUR GIRLFRIEND ARE IN
TOTAL AGREEMENT ABOUT THIS. WITHOUT HER HELP, YOU
WILL FAIL. COUNT ON IT.

THIRD, GET INTO SEVERAL ACCOUNTABILITY RELATION-

SHIPS. THE MOST IMPORTANT ONE IS THE ONE WITH YOUR GIRLFRIEND, BUT ENLIST OTHER FRIENDS TO HELP. GIVE THEM PERMISSION TO ASK YOU ABOUT YOUR SEX LIFE REGULARLY. THEN COMMIT TO TELLING THEM THE TRUTH AND ACCEPTING THEIR ADVICE. ASK THEM TO PRAY HARD FOR YOU.

DON'T DATE NAKED. CLOTHE YOURSELF WITH PRAYER, A COMMITMENT TO PURITY, AND ACCOUNTABILITY. WE ARE OPTIMISTIC THAT YOU WILL BE SUCCESSFUL.

—Mike & Amy

6
staying safe while dating

This is one chapter we wish we didn't have to write. We wish that dating were always a safe experience and that people never took advantage of each other. But we live in the real world, don't we.

Maybe you know people who have been involved in a date rape—either as the victim or as the perpetrator. We sure do.

Maybe you have been the victim of a date rape. Or maybe you have been the perpetrator of a date rape.

We've seen the pain caused in both young men and women, and it's that pain that compels us to write this chapter. Our goal is twofold: to help you prevent a date rape from happening to you, and to give some direction if you've been raped or if you've raped someone.

First, let's be clear about what we mean by date rape. The dictionary defines *date rape* as "rape committed by someone known to the victim."[1] Date rape is different from other kinds of rape in that the perpetrator is a person with whom the victim has had a dating relationship, a person such as a friend or colleague. And because date rape is rape, it is sexual intercourse without consent, sex that is often accompanied by force and sometimes violence.

These are sobering issues, but we feel that if we address them, we can—and you can—light the path to prevention and healing. Again, we're going to talk straight with you: woman to woman and man to man. Amy will start with a story and some wise advice.

AMY SAYS

One time when I was in high school, my parents were off in Atlanta on a business trip. My older sisters happened to be out that evening, but I still never thought twice about inviting Jeremy, a football player I was dating, to visit and share some dessert with me.

When he arrived, we were all alone in the house. Mistake number one.

I was really, really naïve. Mistake number two.

Jeremy, it turned out, wanted more than a second helping of dessert, and it sure wasn't Mom's apple pie. We soon found ourselves on the living room couch, where we began kissing. But then he did something he'd never done before: Jeremy flipped me over on my stomach and sat on my legs. It all happened so fast.

I was about to say something when he put his right hand down the back of my jeans.

At that point, I got really scared. I knew I was not in a

good place. I had a strong football player sitting on my legs, and he was acting as if he was in total control of the situation. I needed to disabuse him of that notion.

"Hey, get off me!" I yelled out as I squirmed to be free. "You've got to leave right now!"

Jeremy acted defensively. "Oh, come on," he said. "I was just kidding."

"No, you are really freaking me out. It's time for you to go."

"Listen, I was just fooling around. I didn't mean anything by that."

"My parents will be home any minute. I think you better go," I repeated.

Jeremy reluctantly got off my legs, grabbed his letterman's jacket, and quickly left the house without saying a word.

I shut the front door and turned the dead bolt. Then I leaned back against the door and breathed a heavy sigh of relief. I had always feared getting raped, and something told me that Jeremy would have done his level best to force himself on me that night. In the weeks and months following that incident, I wondered: *Why in the world did I put myself in that position?*

As I said before—I was naïve. Maybe you are too. We always think date rape happens to the other girl, that she was in the wrong place at the wrong time. That's not entirely true. Date rape can happen anytime, anywhere, if you don't take precautions to protect yourself from compromising situations. You have no idea how possible it is for a young man with raging hormones to get carried away and force himself on a young woman—and steal her virginity in a heartbeat.

Preventing date rape is all about avoiding situations and people that could get you into trouble. Here are some things for you young women to keep in mind:

Know the people you hang out with. How well do you know the person who has been asking you out? What were his past relationships like? What do his friends say about him? What do your friends say about him? Good answers to these questions should not automatically qualify him to be the most trustworthy date in history, but you have to start somewhere.

Back in college I talked to friends about guys they went out with. When one of my girlfriends said, "This guy gives me the creeps," I filed that information away. She wasn't saying that to ruin his reputation but to pass along a friendly tip. If I had a bad experience with a guy or felt that he pressured me, I would warn my friends.

Keep your antennae up. "Trust, but verify," said President Reagan when signing a missile disarmament pact with the Soviet Union years ago. You can be trusting, but it wouldn't hurt to verify a guy's character with people whose opinion you respect.

It's impossible to "profile" someone who might force himself on you, but I would steer away from guys who are cocky, self-centered, selfish, rude to adults, feel as if they own the world, and come across as powerful. Date rape is very much a power thing.

These guys could be influenced by extensive forays into Internet porn, which pumps out the message that when women say no, they really mean yes. These guys could be fueled by out-of-control sexual desires brought on by incessant masturbation. They believe that there's nothing wrong with trying to seduce you, and if you resist, well, that means you want it all the more.

I'm sorry to say that just because a guy says he's a Christian, it doesn't mean he's entirely safe. We've heard too many stories about "good Christian kids" who wouldn't hurt a gypsy moth, but they are hooked by sex and want sex and will do whatever they can to get sex. Just because they're in your student Bible study or sit in church near you every Sunday morning, it doesn't mean they are totally tracking with the Lord. You can never tell what they are thinking—or what they might do when nobody is looking. Not all "Christians" act the way Christians should.

Remember: Don't date naked. Clothe yourself in prayer. Pray about the guy you are dating. Ask God to help you discern whether the person is safe. Then keep your eyes open. If he honors and respects you in the little things, you probably can trust him to honor your physical limits too. Don't ignore warning signs. If the guy does or says inappropriate things to you, confront him about it. If he doesn't respond, you may need to end the relationship.

Know where you're going, and don't be afraid to leave. No one likes to be called a "party pooper" or teased that they are too goody-goody to go to a party. But if you find yourself driven to a boisterous party that you're sure the cops are going to be called in to break up, make noises that you don't want to go in. The time to whine is *before* you step into the party. It's hard to convince your date that you want to leave ten minutes after you arrive: that might put him into a situation where he would lose face, and no one wants to lose face in front of his peers.

"Can't we go to Starbucks instead?" you could ask. Or, "Let's go rent a video." Do something to change the scenery. Find something else to do. The same advice goes for those huge parties in which you don't know the host or many of the participants.

The best alternative is to organize an evening of socializing with your Christian friends. You can have tons of fun and get rowdy without being under the influence.

Stay away from raves and other wild parties. Raves may sound like another dance party, but these energetic all-night happenings are usually staged in rusty-roofed warehouses rented for the evening by "promoters" who turn the venue into a happening place with a huge sound system, banks of strobes and colorful lights, and jive-talking DJs who crank up the volume and the energy on the dance floor. You pay your ten bucks at the door, and you enter a world where there are no rules and plenty of dancing in ways that simulate sexual actions. Couples dip up and down in synchronization—well, you get the picture. This isn't your junior high ice-cream social in the church fellowship hall.

The hundreds or thousands attending the rave usually arrive blitzed, but if they aren't, they soon will be under the influence of some party drug. Inhibitions are history. If you peer into the dark corners of the dilapidated building, you can see couples, well, coupling. So it's not surprising that in such a decadent atmosphere you might have a few dudes scanning the horizon, looking for someone's drink that they can spike with a date-rape drug.

Don't even put yourself in such a situation. I mean—*duh!* If someone invites you to a rave and mentions that no one arrives before midnight, a warning bell should be clanging inside your head. Date rapes happen at night, usually after midnight. That's when your guard should be up.

Think about when and where you go. Date rapes rarely happen at the movies or during Sunday morning church or in the cafeteria or inside the mall. They happen at crazy parties where alcohol and drugs flow.

Again, don't assume that if a party is thrown by Christians, nothing bad will happen. I've attended parties at both Christian colleges and state universities, and sometimes the parties at the Christian colleges were just as wild. Michael and I both observed that some of the kids who were the hardiest partyers came from strict teetotaling homes.

Be on your guard. Dress for success. Put on the belt of accountability, the shoes of honor, and the shield of purity.

Stick to double dating. I know that double dating sounds like something your parents made you do, but it's not a bad idea to double-date two or three times before going out alone with a guy. You may think you can handle any situation that comes up, but don't be so sure. Everything is so sexually stimulated these days, and the expectations of men are high. They expect women to be more sexually provocative and more sexually active. You should look for hints: *What is this guy seeing? What are his expectations of me?*

One hint would be a guy who wants to socially isolate you. The more he can isolate you from your friends and from comfortable surroundings, the more he could be angling for ways to bring on sexual pressure.

Nip advances in the bud. I don't know whether Jeremy would have forced me to have sex, but I didn't want him to stick around just so that I could find out. If someone doesn't act like a total gentleman with you and makes a rash sexual advance, it's time to pull the plug on the evening and ask him to leave. Take one step at a time: first, you need to get out of the bad situation, so politely demand that he vamoose. Then you can tell him later that you don't want to see him again—and explain why. Describe that the way he treats you should be a variation of WWJD (What would Jesus do?), which is, "What would you do if Jesus were here?" Or ask him directly, "Listen, would you be pulling this stuff if Jesus were here with us at this moment?" That should give him pause.

If the unimaginable starts happening, put up a fight. I've sometimes wondered what would have happened if Jeremy had actually started grabbing at my Levis and tried to undress me so that he could force himself on me. What if he hadn't stopped? What would I have done?

That "what if" causes me to shudder to this day. I believe I would have fought off Jeremy with my balled-up fists, and I may have delivered a swift kick where it counted to let him know that I meant business. Once he crossed the line—started undressing me against my will—I would have taken that as a signal that he was not going to stop until he got what he wanted. I believe I would have fought with all my being to protect my body and my future. I do know that my yelling at him—"Hey, get off me!"—put him on the defensive and put me back in control of a potentially threatening situation. Rape counselors suggest that fighting back may not be appropriate in all situations, but in my situation I think it would have helped.

As I look back on that night, I realize that God in his mercy protected me. Pray for that same protection for yourself.

Michael is going to talk with guys about date rape, but I want you females to listen in.

MICHAEL SAYS

Well, guys, let's talk. Like it or not, it's most often the male of the species who perpetrates date rape.

I'm going to talk to you the same way I talked with the guys in my youth group. The last time we discussed date rape, I said to them in the most dead-serious tone I could muster: "Listen, if I ever hear that you forced yourself on a girl, I will personally come after you and—"

I mean it when I say I would have to be physically restrained from doing bodily harm to the guy. I feel very strongly about this. A guy who would rape a woman— even if he convinced himself that she "wanted it"—deserves harsh punishment. Rape is the ultimate violation of a woman, and it causes short-term pain and distress as well as long-term sexual dysfunction, in many cases.

As you can tell, I'm pretty heated about this. Date rape is so dishonoring, so opposite of love. It's self-centered since it's all about taking sexual release at the expense of an unwilling partner. It wasn't that long ago that rape was a capital crime, and for good reason.

Then there are cases that I call "date rape lite." That's when the young man continually pressures his date to have sex. He chips away at her resolve, sometimes working on her for days, weeks, or months until she surrenders her chastity. Guys have been "closing" this deal for decades with the same lines men our fathers' age have used:

- "C'mon, we're in love. I love you, and you love me."
- "I need you to prove your love to me."
- "I love you so much that I can't wait to love you."
- "We're going to get married, so it's okay."
- "Aren't you curious what sex is like?"
- "Just this once."
- "Please, pretty please."

That's right. When all else fails, they beg.

Listen: Don't pressure her, feed her lines, or even drop little hints about how "great" it would be to "make love." This approach agitates me, because it's nothing more than trying to take down a strong and moral person by harassment—until she gives up and gives in to your sexual desires.

I urge you to look at yourself. Hard. Are you an honorable person? Do you honor the young women you date? Do you respect them as people, or do you see them as a key to your sexual satisfaction? Do you respect them enough to honor their physical limits? If you get a little heated and she tries to slow you down, do you listen to her?

Don't be foolish. Don't date naked. Put on honor. Respect yourself and your dating partner. Commit to sexual purity.

Listen, I've been tempted too. I remember times when my hormones raged like a hurricane, and it's only by the grace of God that I didn't go over the edge.

If you can look back on your dating relationship and realize that your hormones rage—sometimes out of control—then place yourself in accountability. Immediately. Admit that you need help. Find some guys, maybe even some older men, who will walk with you and help you stay on track. Don't risk hurting someone because you were too self-focused to get help.

Here's the point I want to leave you with. Guys, you must take the responsibility to say no. Don't for an instant think you can have a little fun by pushing her boundaries, seeing what you can "get" with the thought (and hope) that she'll slam the brakes on going any further.

Is it honoring her for you to test her limits?

No.

Would God be pleased with your behavior?

No, and he's watching, by the way.

One of Amy's young friends, Cara, told me that she and her boyfriend had broken up. When I said, "Oh, I'm sorry to hear that," Cara said, "No, it was a good thing. We both felt as if we were spending too much time together, and frankly, the physical part was getting really hard to resist. We were real committed not to go past kissing."

I hugged Cara. "You are so mature. That is awesome to hear."

Unfortunately, many young women today are more vulnerable to sexual advances than they think. Women who have been rejected by their fathers—who didn't receive love and affection when they grew up because their fathers were not there or not involved—will welcome almost anyone's showering them with love and attention. Amy says that nine out of the ten girls she counsels—those who were rejected by their fathers—have been involved in promiscuous relationships.

If You've Been Involved in Date Rape

The next few paragraphs are primarily for young women who have been victims of a date rape and for young men who have been the perpetrators. If you are neither of those, we want you to read this section anyway, because reading it may help you bring healing to someone in either category.

Let's start with the females. First, we want to say how sorry we are that you were violated. We've talked with enough people to begin to know the pain, shame, guilt, and devastation you probably feel. As we discuss these hard issues, remember that God loves you, and he is the Redeemer. He can bring light out of darkness, healing out of hurt. Some of you will have already thought about much of what we say here, but others of you have not talked much about your rape, and it will help you to think about what we say.

1. You are not to blame. Date rape, by definition, is sex that is forced on someone, sex that is "taken" without consent. You did not invite that action. Don't blame yourself and beat yourself up. The perpetrator is responsible for the action. You may be carrying a false sense of guilt. Release it to God, and find freedom.

2. Don't hide. Some young women have felt such shame at being raped that they have not told anyone, and as a result they have cut themselves off from help and have unnecessarily carried an enormous burden. Talk *appropriately* with mature people about the rape. We say *appropriately* because some girls have gone to the other extreme and told anyone who would listen about the incident; they seem to have a need to wear a *V* for victim. Also, don't hide in an attempt to protect the perpetrator; he needs to face what he's done.

3. Get help. Rape has violated you—physically, emotionally, and spiritually. The fact that it was date rape means that your trust was also violated by someone you know. See a doctor for any physical help you might need. We strongly urge you to get counseling. Dealing with the many emotional aspects of date rape is a complex process. A skilled, compassionate counselor will help you walk the road to healing and wholeness. Talk to your pastor, a therapist, or other mature adult. Find a support group, if possible. There's such comfort in working through difficult situations with people who know from firsthand experience what you are facing.

4. Deal with the perpetrator. After you address some of your immediate needs, you need to deal with the perpetrator. Rape is a crime. You might be wise to report the perpetrator to the police. If you do this, the sooner after the incident you file the report, the better. If you were actively dating the perpetrator at the time of the rape, we suggest you break up with the guy. Put distance between you and the person who took what wasn't his to take. If possible, confront the person about what he did. But don't do this casually. Remember, rape is a violent crime. Talk with a counselor about how you might confront the perpetrator. You might want to write a letter (which you may or may not choose to send) to let him know the extent to which he damaged you. After some time of healing, you will be ready to forgive the perpetrator. We are not suggesting that this is an easy or a one-time thing. But release him to God's judgment, and free yourself from the bonds you will feel if you hold on to bitterness or resentment.

5. Give yourself time. Recovering from rape is not an easy process. Don't expect your distress to be over in a week or two, or even a month or two. Healing takes time. Be patient with yourself.

6. Find hope in God. God, through his Son Jesus, is the Redeemer. He not only redeemed us from our sinfulness but also redeems the most difficult situations and eventually turns them into good. He shines light on the dark situations of our lives. Through his Holy Spirit, the Comforter, he will walk with you as you recover from the rape.

Now a few words to those of you who were the perpetrators in a date rape.

1. Admit your guilt. Some of you are taking a deep breath here. A few of you have never faced what you did. Now is the time to do that. Saying to yourself, *I committed a rape*, is a very difficult thing. But you must do it. This is the "I was wrong" part of the process.[2] And you can do it because God is a forgiving God. We know men who never faced up to the fact that they perpetrated a date rape when they were younger, and it is eating them up.

2. Confess your guilt to God. Once you admit that what you did was wrong, confess it to God. This is the "I'm sorry" part of the process. This is also the freeing part of the process. We can afford to confess the most horrible deeds to God because we know he already knows about them, and he has already paid the price to forgive us for our sin.

3. Ask for and accept God's forgiveness. This is the "please forgive me" part of the process. Believe God when he says that "if we confess our sins to him, he is faithful and just to forgive us and to cleanse us from every wrong" (1 John 1:9). What a wonderful promise. Accept it. Act as if it is true.

4. Deal with the victim. Once you have gotten things straightened out between you and God, you need to think of the victim. We hear you taking another deep breath here. We suggest that you talk with a counselor or other trusted adult about this part. You must deal with the victim both for your sake and for hers. Trust us when we say that what you did wounded her deeply. For your sake, you need to face this part of what you did and acknowledge it to yourself. For her sake, she needs to hear that you realize that what you did was wrong, that you are sorry for what you did, that you ask for her forgiveness, and that you have committed yourself to never acting that way again. Pray about this part. You may decide to write her a letter. You may decide to talk with her; if you do, we suggest that you do it with a third party present, ideally a counselor. The goal here is not to win her back. The goal is not necessarily a reconciliation between the two of you. The goal is to help her in the healing process.

5. Put away your sin. This is the "I will never do it again" part of the process. The word *repent* means to have a change of heart, to turn around and go in the opposite direction. You need to turn from your behavior and walk the other way—away from sexual episodes, away from self-centeredness, away from sin. And you'll need help to do this, especially if you feel that you are struggling with sexual addictions. Talk with a pastor, a counselor, a mature Christian man. Find brothers who will be able to pray with you and hold you accountable to this decision. Remember God's promise that he will not only forgive but also cleanse you from every wrong.

6. Put on some new clothes. As you go into your next dating relationship, don't even think about dating naked.

We want you to "stand firm against all strategies and tricks of the Devil." In order to do that, "clothe yourselves with the Lord Jesus Christ, and do not think about how to gratify the desires of the sinful nature" (Romans 13:14, NIV). Put on the robe of prayer, the belt of accountability, the shoes of honor. Take up the shield of sexual purity. And take hope. God will walk with you. He will honor your desire to walk with integrity.

AMY SAYS: Let me say a few words about the Internet and its impact on dating. While the Internet is an invaluable tool for all of us, it can also be dangerous. Sexual predators stalk the Internet just as much as the poorly lit warehouses that are home to out-of-control raves. Scrolling through chat rooms is not the ideal way to find a date for Friday night. People can pretend to be whoever they want to be in a chat room.

Be wary of the dating Web sites. If you are going to use them at all, stay at the Christian dating sites, many of which are quite legitimate and quite helpful. One of them, eharmony.com, is associated with Dr. Neil Clark Warren, a Christian counselor and author of *Finding the Love of Your Life*. The service seems to be geared to those seriously looking to get married rather than just going out on a casual date.

Check around, and ask friends what their experiences have been with Christian dating sites. Please know that these dating sites are fee based. Eharmony.com, for instance, costs $49 a month (or $249 a year), while others, such as ChristianCafe and the Singles Christian Network, charge around $20 to $25 a month.

A second danger of the Internet is the availability of pornography. You are the first generation to grow up with pornography at your fingertips. And it's free. You don't have to be eighteen to view it, and you certainly don't have to drive to a seedy part of town in a raincoat to buy some glossy magazines filled with pictures of naked women and naked couples cavorting.

MICHAEL SAYS

That's why pornography scares me. As an aside, did you know that pornography is the number one common denominator among men sitting on death row in our nation's prisons? It's the only common denominator! Every person on death row has had a problem with pornography or was deeply involved with the stuff.

This toxic waste is the most dangerous thing infiltrating our society today. Forget terrorists, forget divorce. Pornography is warping millions of guys' minds and encouraging them to "act out" what they see on the computer. If you're around porn much, you're convinced that women want sex any time of the day or night; that when they say no, they really mean yes; that the world is populated with incredibly built women with large chests, tiny waists, and full thighs; and that a woman's basic role in life is to give sexual pleasure to men. Wrong on all counts!

Porn distorts the mind. It perverts the soul. It makes you want to have more, see more. I counseled a young boy who was getting into a lot of trouble with his stepdad. His mother was stressed out, and the boy was starting to flunk school. It turned out that he had gotten into looking at pornography on the computer. It just made him want to have sex more and more. He didn't have a girlfriend, so he called the first anonymous woman who came into his head—the operator.

"Ah, yes, I was calling to see if you would have sex with me. I really need to have sex."

"Excuse me?"

Thank God the operator had the good sense to keep him on the line until she could reach the police. At one o'clock in the morning, a detective from the vice squad knocked on the parents' front door.

"Does Dan Jeffreys live here?" the patrolman asked the startled stepfather.

"Yes," he replied. "He's in his bedroom asleep."

"No, we think he was on the phone soliciting an operator for sex."

Please, whether you've had a whiff of this stuff or know you're in way over your head, get help.

MICHAEL'S STRAIGHT TALK ABOUT PORNOGRAPHY

1. Pornography is evil. It will poison your mind, emotions, and soul.

2. Pornography is powerful. It will consume you.

3. Pornography is antithetical to honor and purity. It will corrode you.

4. Pornography is addictive. It will obsess you.

5. Don't view pornography. Period. Stand firm against all strategies and tricks of the Devil.

6. Don't fight it alone. Form an accountability group to keep your mind clean. Cover yourself with the robe of prayer, and put on the belt of accountability.

7. Don't fantasize about what you've seen. Honor God's creation of the human body, and honor women by not seeing them as sexual objects.

8. If you're already hooked, confess it to God and others, ask for forgiveness, repent (turn your behavior around), and look daily to the help of the Holy Spirit and of other godly men.

Don't ever underestimate the power of pornography. I remember when I was in graduate school at Wheaton College; I was married and the father of two kids. I had never been into porn. Sure, I had looked at a few *Playboys* growing up, but I kept that stuff at arm's length.

Then one night I had a paper due on teenagers. I started my research by doing a Google search and typing in the word *teenagers.* I clicked on one of the first listings, and boom—there it was. Pornography.

It was so easy. In the weeks after that, I struggled. Occasionally I would allow myself a quick "visit." One night I thought about what I was doing, and it scared me. It scared me that I had so easily slid down the slippery slope. It scared me that the images had so much power over me. I faced my sin, confessed it to God, and received his forgiveness. Then I repented and made some changes to safeguard my behavior.

First, I realized that the temptation was stronger because my computer was downstairs in the basement, and I was down there all by myself. It was easy to check out a site and have no one know.

Second, I talked to my therapist. Being in therapy was part of my graduate training to become a therapist, so I discussed my struggle with the counselor. She helped me look at what I was doing and what I needed to do to make sure I didn't continue.

Third, I confessed my transgression to Amy. She was amazing about it. She did not shame me. She did not pull back from me sexually. She helped me put some safeguards in place. When we moved back to Branson, I put my office in a family room for all to see. And that's the accountability I have needed.

Some men I know have installed blocking software to screen out pornographic sites, but that's just a Band-Aid over a wound that needs surgery. Blocking software is better than nothing, but those porn sites multiply like rabbits, and it's impossible to keep up.

AMY SAYS

I recently talked to a man who was involved with Internet porn, and he said blocking software doesn't work well. He has had to take more drastic measures to ensure that he doesn't go back to visiting pornographic sites.

I had no idea how powerful the pull of pornography is until Michael talked with me about his temptation. While I was surprised to know that my husband struggled, I was pleased when he said he was taking definite steps to ensure that he didn't make that mistake again. Pornography is evil. That's clear to me. Not only do I hate what it says about the female body, but I hate what it does to men. I pray for my husband, and I do whatever I can to help him protect himself.

It's hard to explain what pornography does to a person. It's kind of like forming calluses on your hands. First, a blister forms, and there's a high sensitivity to that, but after a while, that blister becomes a callus. For you to feel anything, you really have to scratch that callus because your skin becomes tougher and tougher.

It's the same way with pornography. Guys find that what used to thrill them no longer does the trick. They keep going back for more and more and more. When they see women topless, then they want to see them totally naked. And when they see them totally naked, they want to see them performing sex acts. And you can only imagine where it goes from there.

I've heard about date-rape drugs. Are they a serious threat?

—**Worried**

DEAR WORRIED,

YES, THEY ARE. SEXUAL PREDATORS USE SEVERAL KINDS OF DRUGS, WHICH THEY SLIP TO UNSUSPECTING FEMALES. IT COULD ALL HAPPEN IF YOU INNOCENTLY SAY YES WHEN OFFERED A DRINK AT A PARTY, DISCO, RAVE—WHATEVER. THE GUY OFTEN HAS A VISINE BOTTLE WITH GHB—A DRUG WHOSE INITIALS STAND FOR GAMMA HYDROXYBUTYRATE, BUT COULD STAND FOR "GRIEVOUS HARM TO THE BODY." HE STRIKES UP A CONVERSATION, AND WHEN YOU'RE NOT LOOKING, SQUEEZES A FEW DROPS OF THE COLORLESS AND ODORLESS GHB INTO YOUR DRINK.

GHB IS SCARY STUFF. IT WORKS FAST, AND IT'S EFFECTIVE. AT FIRST, YOU'LL FEEL SEXUALLY AGGRESSIVE AND MAY EVEN COME ON TO THE GUY. BUT THEN YOU'LL BEGIN FEELING QUEASY, AND IT WON'T BE LONG UNTIL YOU PASS OUT. THE GUY WITH THE VISINE BOTTLE KNOWS ALL THESE TELLTALE SIGNS. WHEN YOU START COMPLAINING ABOUT FEELING SICK, HE'LL SUGGEST TAKING YOU OUTSIDE FOR SOME "FRESH AIR." THE NEXT THING YOU KNOW, YOU'LL WAKE UP HOURS LATER UNDER THE FIRE ESCAPE. THAT'S IF YOU WAKE UP AT ALL. SOME YOUNG WOMEN HAVE OVERDOSED AFTER SIPPING SODAS LACED WITH GHB.

GHB USED TO BE SOLD IN HEALTH FOOD STORES AS A GROWTH HORMONE STIMULANT OR A SLEEP DISORDER MEDICINE. WHEN KIDS GOT WIND OF THE CRAZY THINGS IT CAN DO TO YOU, THE FOOD AND DRUG ADMINISTRATION YANKED IT OFF THE SHELVES IN 1991. THAT MERELY PUSHED THE DRUG UNDERGROUND. PEOPLE CAN ORDER GHB KITS OFF THE INTERNET AND WHIP SOME UP IN THEIR BATHTUBS.

GHB IS BAD, REALLY BAD, AND IT'S REPLACED ROHYP-

NOL—OR "ROOFIES"—AS THE DATE-RAPE DRUG OF CHOICE.
"ROOFIES" AND A DATE-RAPE COUSIN CALLED CLONAZEPAM
ARE CHEAP; THEY CAN BE HAD ON THE STREET FOR $1,
WHICH IS WHY THEY'RE HYPED AS "DOLLAR DATE" DRUGS.

TO AVOID THE THREAT OF DATE-RAPE DRUGS, STAY AWAY
FROM PLACES WHERE IT MIGHT BE USED, AND KEEP YOUR
EYES OPEN FOR GUYS WHO MIGHT BE SEXUAL PREDATORS.

—Mike & Amy

Dear Mike & Amy,

I learned that my boyfriend is into pornography, and it scares me. What should I do? Should
I break up with him? Should I be patient?

—Scared

Dear Scared,

I (MICHAEL) USED TO KNOW GUYS WHO WOULD HAVE
PORN-WATCHING PARTIES WITH THEIR OTHER BUDDIES!
YOU DON'T WANT TO BE ANYWHERE NEAR A GUY WHO THINKS
PORNOGRAPHY IS "FUNNY," "COOL," OR "NO BIG DEAL."
THIS KIND OF INVOLVEMENT WITH PORNOGRAPHY NEEDS TO
BE DEALT WITH IMMEDIATELY. WE SUGGEST YOU BREAK OFF
THE RELATIONSHIP.

YOU ARE FAR TOO VALUABLE TO BE WITH SOME GUY WHO
CLEARLY PLACES A LOW VALUE ON WOMEN. YOU DON'T NEED
THIS GUY. ALL YOU REALLY NEED ON THIS EARTH IS
CHRIST! IF YOUR BOYFRIEND IS TRULY "INTO" PORNOG-
RAPHY, ALL YOUR PATIENCE IS GOING TO DO IS CAUSE
YOU EXTRA PAIN AND SUFFERING FROM A DOOMED-
FROM-THE-START RELATIONSHIP.

TRUST YOUR FEAR IN THIS RELATIONSHIP. MANY TIMES
WE WANT TO IGNORE OUR FEAR BECAUSE WE BELIEVE THE
LIES FROM THE MEDIA AND OUR PEERS THAT WE ARE PRUD-
ISH, NAÏVE, OR SOMETHING ELSE IF WE DON'T TOLERATE
PORNOGRAPHY. FEAR IS A GOD-GIVEN RESPONSE TO SITUA-

TIONS THAT CAN BE HARMFUL TO OUR BODY OR SOUL. YOUR FEAR, IF IGNORED, COULD END UP HURTING YOU.

—Mike & Amy

Dear Mike & Amy,

I'm a student at a Christian college, and I'm really struggling with Internet pornography. Several months ago I vowed I would never look at it again, but I have slipped several times. I feel so guilty. Can you help me?

—Hooked

DEAR HOOKED,

WE'RE GLAD TO HEAR THAT YOU ALREADY RECOGNIZE THAT YOU HAVE A PROBLEM. THAT'S AN INCREDIBLY IMPORTANT FIRST STEP. YOU'VE EVEN TRIED TO STOP. THAT'S A GOOD SIGN TOO. IT MEANS YOUR HEART IS POINTED IN THE RIGHT DIRECTION. AND YOU REALIZE THE INCREDI-BLE PULL THE PORNOGRAPHY HAS ON YOU. AS WE'VE SAID IN THIS CHAPTER: PORNOGRAPHY IS EVIL. WE ARE CON-VINCED THAT IT IS ONE OF THE ENEMY'S POWERFUL STRATEGIES TO INFECT THE SOULS OF MEN. AS A RESULT, WE HAVE TO FIGHT FIRE WITH FIRE—THE FIRE OF SATAN WITH THE FIRE OF GOD'S SPIRIT.

LET US OFFER SOME PRACTICAL STEPS THAT MAY HELP. IF YOU'VE NOT ALREADY DONE SO, TRY THESE THINGS:

1. CONFESS YOUR STRUGGLE TO GOD, AND SURRENDER YOURSELF FULLY TO HIM.
2. PRAY LIKE YOU'VE NEVER PRAYED BEFORE. PUT ON THE ROBE OF PRAYER.
3. ASK OTHERS TO HELP YOU. FORM AN ACCOUNTABIL-ITY GROUP OF MEN WHO WILL PRAY FOR YOU AND ASK YOU REGULARLY—SEVERAL TIMES A DAY, IF NECESSARY—HOW YOU ARE DOING. PUT ON THE BELT OF ACCOUNTABILITY.

4. GET BLOCKING SOFTWARE FOR YOUR COMPUTER.
5. USE THE COMPUTER ONLY WHEN YOU ARE OUT IN THE OPEN, WHERE OTHERS CAN SEE YOU.
6. WRITE YOURSELF NOTES AND TAPE THEM TO YOUR MONITOR. TRY NOTES LIKE THESE: "I WILL KEEP MY MIND PURE." "THINK ABOUT THINGS THAT ARE PURE AND LOVELY AND ADMIRABLE" (PHILIPPIANS 4:8). "I WILL NOT LOOK AT PORN." USE WHATEVER PHRASES ARE MEANINGFUL TO YOU.
7. THE BIBLE SAYS, "IF YOUR EYE CAUSES YOU TO SIN, GOUGE IT OUT AND THROW IT AWAY. IT IS BETTER TO ENTER HEAVEN HALF BLIND THAN TO HAVE TWO EYES AND BE THROWN INTO HELL" (MATTHEW 18:9). WHILE WE ARE NOT SUGGESTING THAT YOU GOUGE OUT YOUR EYE, WE DO SUGGEST THAT YOU TAKE DRASTIC MEASURES. MAYBE IN YOUR CASE IT'S, "IF YOUR COMPUTER LEADS YOU INTO SIN, GET RID OF IT." WE KNOW OF GUYS WHO HAVE DONE THAT FOR SEVERAL MONTHS IN ORDER TO BREAK THE HABIT. DO WHAT YOU NEED TO DO. YOUR SOUL IS AT STAKE.
8. NOT VIEWING THE PORNOGRAPHY IS NOT ENOUGH. COMMIT YOURSELF TO GUARDING YOUR MIND FROM FANTASIZING ABOUT WHAT YOU HAVE ALREADY SEEN. JUST SHUT THE DOOR.

WE PRAY THAT YOU FIND VICTORY IN YOUR STRUGGLE WITH GUILT. AND REMEMBER, "THE LORD IS MERCIFUL AND GRACIOUS; HE IS SLOW TO GET ANGRY AND FULL OF UNFAILING LOVE. HE WILL NOT CONSTANTLY ACCUSE YOU OR REMAIN ANGRY FOREVER. HE HAS NOT PUNISHED YOU FOR ALL YOUR SINS, NOR DOES HE DEAL WITH YOU AS YOU DESERVE. FOR HIS UNFAILING LOVE TOWARD YOU, WHO FEAR HIM, IS AS GREAT AS THE HEIGHT OF THE HEAVENS ABOVE THE EARTH. HE HAS REMOVED YOUR REBELLIOUS ACTS AS FAR AWAY FROM YOU AS THE EAST IS FROM THE WEST. THE LORD IS LIKE A FATHER TO YOU, TENDER AND

COMPASSIONATE, FOR HE UNDERSTANDS HOW WEAK YOU ARE; HE KNOWS YOU ARE ONLY DUST" (PARAPHRASE OF PSALM 103:8-14).

—Mike & Amy

7
maintaining emotional boundaries

MICHAEL SAYS

When I graduated from Scottsdale Christian Academy High School, Stacy (the fun-loving girl I splashed with watermelon on our first date) and I were still very much an "item" on campus. We weren't voted "Class Couple," since she was a grade ahead of me, but we had a *great* relationship and enjoyed so much fun together.

Although we were close—and I saw us marrying one day—we never considered attending the same college together. I think we both wanted to explore life outside the Valley of the Sun: meet other people, date others, but always assuming that in the end, we would become Mr. and Mrs. Michael Smalley. All of this was unsaid, of course, because we were young and immature, but that's how both of us felt.

So we went our separate ways. When I was a high school senior, Stacy flew off to Bethel College in St. Paul, Minnesota, and the following year I headed for the activity-rich Baylor University in Waco, Texas.

You know me—I had a good time from the first night I checked into Martin Hall, making friends, acting crazy, and checking out the Dr Pepper Museum in downtown Waco. Because I was still interested in Stacy, I didn't look around too much for anyone else to date. Consequently, except for a couple of whirlwind relationships, I experienced a long dry spell that lasted well into my junior year.

Throughout my college years I kept in touch with Stacy by calling her every few months. Our relationship was nothing serious, but I wanted to keep things going because I still thought she was The One. When we came home from college for summer vacations, we picked up where we had left off. The embers of our close relationship may have burned low, but that was fine with both of us. We figured that someday after graduation, we would reignite our love for each other and then we would tie the knot.

Early in my junior year at Baylor, I received one of those periodic phone calls from Stacy.

"Hey, can I talk to you?" she asked in that perky way of hers.

"Sure. What's going on?"

"Well, I wanted you to be the first to know."

"Know what?"

"That I'm engaged."

"Engaged? You've got to be kidding me!" I was shocked. "How did that happen?"

"Well, Mark and I met in a communications class last spring, and things moved pretty fast. Now we are getting married."

"I'm happy for you, Stacy." I paused. "So are you calling me to find out how I feel about your getting engaged?"

"Well, I'm not sure exactly why I'm calling you."

"To be totally honest, I am shocked. I really thought we would get together someday and get married."

For the longest time I heard total silence on the phone line. I knew what she was thinking: *Great. Now I have two guys asking me to get married.* "I did not expect this," she whispered.

"Sorry, but that's how I feel. You are a great person, someone who would be a lot of fun to be married to."

"Let me think about it," she said. "I'll call you back in a few days."

The next night, I went out to dinner with the Baylor yell team at Ryan's Steakhouse. On this fairly festive evening, I was surrounded by a covey of gorgeous-looking women, including Amy. I opened up and told them about my conversation with Stacy.

"You are unbelievable," gushed Mary Lynn, one of the cheerleaders. "That is so insane. You are so gutsy. Listen, Michael—don't hold back, and we'll pray for you. I hope it works out with Stacy."

A week later I still hadn't heard from Stacy, so I decided to call and learn my fate. "I kind of hoped that I would have heard from you by now with an answer," I said.

"Yeah, I'm sorry, but I'm going to stick with this guy," she said.

What was there left to say, except good-bye? When I returned the phone to its cradle, waves of devastation swept over me. I felt worthless, like a sack of trash tossed overboard. Her rejection was a real kick in the teeth.

As horrible as I felt that day, I think it would have been far worse if I had not maintained some emotional boundaries in the dating relationship. You see, I had never whispered to Stacy the three simple words: "I love you."

Some of you may be thinking that if I *had* said the words, maybe Stacy would have known how I felt about her and wouldn't have dated someone else. I disagree. Stacy knew what I thought of her.

Based on how I treated Stacy, how I respected her, and how I honored the relationship, she knew she was special to me and that we could have a future together. What helped with this commitment was that Stacy and I were on the same page. We talked about saying "I love you." She agreed that we should put boundaries on those words.

We agreed to that because I believe people use those three words far too casually. Too many young people start dating hot and heavy, begin eating every meal together, sharing every *Friends* episode together, and the next thing you know, they're locking eyes and saying, "I love you."

Uttering that phrase is crossing an emotional boundary—the Rubicon of love. Like toothpaste squeezed out of a tube, those words are impossible to put back in once they come out of your mouth. When you say "I love you," you are acting like a married couple, and the reality is that you are *not* married.

Which brings me to my point: I recommend that you do not say "I love you" until you are engaged to be married. Some of you may think that is a foolish warning, but I'd like you to think about it seriously. I waited until Amy and I were officially engaged before I said "I love you" to her, and I will never regret it.

If you've already spoken the "I love you" into the relationship, then the stakes have been raised sky high. All your emotional chips have been pushed to the center of the table. Where do you go from there?

And how are you going to feel if you get dumped? That's when you think, *But I thought you loved me!* Yes, your dating partner said those words, and you believed them. And that's why you hurt so much.

I wish the English language were like Greek when it comes to the word *love*. The Greeks have four words for various kinds of love:

- *storge*, which refers to family love
- *agape*, which refers to unconditional, unselfish, and undeserved love
- *philia*, which refers to friendship love
- *eros*, which refers to romantic love

The distinctions are not so clear in the English language. We use the same word *love* to describe everything from the pedestrian ("I love your eye shadow") to the ultraserious ("I love you so much, Cyndi. Thanks for agreeing to marry me.").

Wouldn't it be great if our language had separate words for various meanings? Then we could communicate to dating partners that we love them with a friendship love and possibly even with an unselfish, undeserved love.

Given the limitation of the English language, it's hardly surprising that our culture has cheapened the use of the word *love*. Our media role models—actors and actresses in films and TV shows—say "I love you" on the first date. (Or do they do that after they have sex at her place on the evening of their first date?)

Even among friends, we yell out "Love you!" Let's agree that the phrase has become shopworn, hackneyed, and sucked dry of any emotional meaning, which is why our challenge to you is for you to wait until you are engaged before saying "I love you" to the person you have pledged to marry.

So what should you say? How about some of these phrases:

- "I care about you a lot."
- "I like you a lot."
- "You are so special to me."

- "You are an incredible person."
- "I really enjoy being with you."

Those phrases convey positive emotion yet suggest that your feelings will continue to grow and mature.

AMY SAYS

Girls, you need to guard your hearts too. We females are just as guilty for saying too much in the heat of passion. Once we've shared our hearts by saying "I love you," we become emotionally bonded, whether we mean to or not. And when guys say "I love you" to us, we struggle with that because it affects our emotions.

We are the more emotional creature of the two sexes. Men tend to think more logically and not as emotionally. We are also more relational than guys. We are always aware of where a relationship is at, while guys can be clueless at times. For example, when women are on a date, they are often thinking things such as, *We seem to be hitting it off well tonight*, or *He seems to want to be closer than before*, or *I think it's time for another DTR (define the relationship) talk*. When guys date, they are aware of the immediate situation. And when females start to launch into a talk to define the relationship, guys are confused, thinking, *Why do we have to talk about the relationship?*

If you get into a dating relationship that looks promising, that looks as if this could be it, you could handle it like this:

Your dating partner: "I was thinking, Sweetie, of how special you have become to me since we met each other. I just really want you to know that I—"

You: "Listen, let me stop you right here, Honey. I think I know what you're going to say because those same feelings have been swirling around my heart. Look, I want you to know that I really care for you. I'm excited about our relationship, but I don't believe in saying 'I love you' unless you're the person I marry, and we're not there yet. I'm saving the saying of 'I love you' for the person I do marry. We're going in a great direction together, but let's keep that sacred, okay?"

It wouldn't hurt for you to build some other emotional boundaries into your budding relationship as well. The first boundary is not spending too much time together like a married couple. You don't have to eat *every* meal together. In fact, you shouldn't, just as you shouldn't go on long vacations together. Another no-no would be having your date spend the night on your living room couch. I don't care if you sleep inside a bank vault

You know she ~~loves~~ *likes* you when . . .

- she puts her arm around your waist as you walk together.
- she allows you to see her without her makeup on.
- she makes you a homemade apple pie.
- she says, "Hey, do you want to watch that big football game together tomorrow afternoon?"

while he's out on the couch; having that close proximity during bedtime creates an emotional closeness and drives you emotionally deeper and more together.

You also push emotional boundaries by spending too much money on each other. Buying each other expensive gifts—or an extravagant "promise" ring—

You know he ~~loves~~ *likes* you when . . .

- he gives up an afternoon of watching his favorite football team on TV so that the two of you can do something together.
- he cooks a great meal at your place and does the cleanup.
- he brings you flowers.
- he sends you a thoughtful e-mail each morning.
- he says, "Hey, I know what we could do! We could go shopping at the mall!"

also promotes emotional bonding. If you do this, you can end up feeling as if you have backed each other into an emotional corner because you have "invested" too much money into the relationship for the other person to say that he or she wants to break up.

A final word of advice: If you're Instant Messaging with your beau, watch what you write as well. Words, as they say, mean things, and your typed-out words can carry extraordinary power. But repeat-typing "I love you" a zillion times can also water down the meaning of your sentiment.

It's best to maintain a reserve—to keep some of your emotions in check. Don't worry. If your relationship progresses to the altar, you will have plenty of opportunities to express your love to your spouse.

Dear Mike & Amy,

I've been dating the same guy for three years now. How do I know if he's the one?

—Eager to decide

DEAR EAGER,

WE HOPE THAT YOU'VE LEARNED FROM THIS BOOK THAT YOU NEED A LIST OF THE QUALITIES YOU WANT IN A SPOUSE. HOW DOES HE COMPARE TO YOUR LIST?

IF YOUR LIST IS COMPLETE AND IF YOU ARE HONEST WITH YOURSELF, YOU SHOULD BE ABLE TO DETERMINE IF HE IS THE ONE.

IF YOU'RE STILL ASKING "IS HE THE ONE?" AFTER THREE YEARS OF DATING, THEN WE'D START TO QUESTION IF HE IS THE GUY YOU SHOULD MARRY. WE'RE NOT SAYING THERE IS SOME MAGICAL FORMULA, BUT THREE YEARS IS A LONG TIME TO GET TO KNOW SOMEONE. IF YOU'RE STILL NOT CONFIDENT, THEN MAYBE YOU HAVEN'T BEEN HONEST WITH YOURSELF AND THE RELATIONSHIP.

IF YOUR BOYFRIEND DOESN'T MATCH YOUR LIST IN A FEW SIGNIFICANT AREAS AND THINGS HAVEN'T CHANGED IN THREE YEARS, THEN YOU NEED TO FACE THE REALITY AND BREAK OFF THE RELATIONSHIP. EVEN THOUGH THAT SEEMS HARD, IT'S SO MUCH BETTER TO BREAK OFF A DAT-ING RELATIONSHIP THAN AN ENGAGEMENT OR MARRIAGE RELATIONSHIP.

BE HONEST WITH YOURSELF. MANY WOMEN TRY TO FORCE GUYS INTO WHAT THEY WANT TO HAVE AND REFUSE TO LOOK AT WHAT THEY'VE GOT. I (AMY) MADE THIS MISTAKE WITH JEFF. HE DIDN'T MATCH ALL THE QUALITIES ON MY LIST, BUT I SPENT A LOT OF YEARS TRYING TO FORCE HIM INTO THEM UNTIL THE RELATIONSHIP FINALLY BLEW UP.

AND REMEMBER TO PRAY ABOUT THIS VERY IMPORTANT DECISION. ASK GOD TO SHOW YOU WHAT YOU NEED IN A

MARRIAGE PARTNER. THEN DON'T SETTLE FOR ANYTHING
LESS.

—Mike & Amy

Dear Mike & Amy,

I'm a sophomore at a Christian college, and I'm
upset that so many of my friends are getting engaged already. From my perspective, some of
them barely know the people they are intending
to live with for the rest of their lives. When I
mentioned my concern to a few of them, they said
that they felt that if they didn't act now, they
would be left behind. That didn't seem like a
healthy perspective. What do you think?

—Upset

Dear Upset,

WE AGREE WITH YOU. IT'S NOT HEALTHY TO JUMP INTO
ENGAGEMENT AND MARRIAGE QUICKLY OR TO GET ENGAGED
BECAUSE YOU DON'T WANT TO BE LEFT BEHIND.

MARRIAGE TO THE RIGHT PERSON IS AN INEXPRESSIBLY
WONDERFUL THING. BUT MARRIAGE TO THE WRONG PERSON
IS MISERY—OR WORSE. PEOPLE NEED TO TAKE THEIR TIME
TO MAKE THIS DECISION—ONE OF THE MOST IMPORTANT DE-
CISIONS OF THEIR LIVES. AS WE'VE SAID IN THIS BOOK,
GETTING TO KNOW EACH OTHER FULLY IS VERY IMPORTANT.

PEOPLE ALSO MOVE INTO ENGAGEMENT AND MARRIAGE TOO
QUICKLY IF THEY DON'T HAVE SOUND EMOTIONAL BOUND-
ARIES. JUST AS GIVING TOO MUCH PHYSICALLY CAN RUIN
A RELATIONSHIP, GIVING TOO MUCH EMOTIONALLY CAN
ALSO LEAD TO DISASTER. COUPLES NEED TO TAKE IT
SLOWLY. WE'VE SEEN PEOPLE LIKE THE ONES YOU MEN-
TION, COUPLES WHO FORGE DEEP EMOTIONAL BONDS THAT
ARE NOT APPROPRIATE FOR DATING. THEY RUSH INTO

ENGAGEMENT ONLY TO FIND OUT THAT THEIR EMOTIONAL BONDS WERE BUILT ON A VERY UNSTABLE FOUNDATION.

IF YOU REALLY WANT TO HELP YOUR FRIENDS, THEN LOVINGLY ENCOURAGE THEM INTO PREMARITAL COUNSELING. IT SOUNDS AS IF YOU'RE WORRIED THEY ARE RUSHING INTO THE WRONG RELATIONSHIP. PREMARITAL COUNSELING IS DESIGNED TO HELP COUPLES REALISTICALLY EVALUATE THEIR RELATIONSHIP. PREMARITAL COUNSELING PROGRAMS LIKE PREPARE, BY DR. DAVID OLSON, HAVE A 10 PERCENT BREAK-UP RATE AFTER A COUPLE GOES THROUGH THE PROGRAM. OUR MINISTRY, THE SMALLEY RELATIONSHIP CENTER, HAS A ONE-DAY ENGAGED ENRICHMENT PROGRAM THAT UTILIZES DR. OLSON'S TEST.

—Mike & Amy

8

what if mr. or ms. right turns out to be all wrong?

Finding Mr. or Ms. Right is an important process, and we hope that some of the things we've talked about in this book will help you find that special person with whom you will spend the rest of your life.

But what if you have doubts? What if the person you are dating turns out to be Mr. or Ms. Wrong? What can you do?

If you are having some serious doubts, step back and take a second look. The worst thing you could do is put your head in the sand and pretend that nothing is wrong. And don't be like the people in the letter at the end of the last chapter—rushing into things because they don't want the marriage train to leave the station without them. Take your time.

AMY SAYS

But how will you know if you need to break off the relationship? We have a few questions that may help, then Michael will offer a few good reasons why you might need to call it a day.

Have you prayed about the situation? Remember, don't date naked. Pray about the relationship. Should you move forward? Should you walk away? God cares about your relationships. He wants you to be in relationships that help you grow and mature, relationships that help you serve him and others.

Have you checked your Qualities List? Now that you know your dating partner better, how does he or she measure up to your Qualities List? Is he or she the person you want to spend the rest of your life with? If you see glaring deficits, face the facts. Don't make the same mistake I did. Check your list, and act on what you know is right.

Is the relationship unhealthy? An unhealthy dating relationship can lead to an unhealthy marriage. If your relationship is not helping you grow—as an individual and as a couple—in clearly positive ways, you may have reason to end the relationship. Here are a few no-brainers.

- Don't stay in the relationship if the person is seriously disrespectful or at all abusive to you—verbally, physically, or sexually. Get out.

- Don't stay in the relationship if the person has a weak or nonexistent commitment to Christ. We've already discussed the situation of dating non-Christians and told you how we feel about that. But what if you start dating someone who knows you are a Christian, knows that Christ and church are important to your life, but is faking interest in or dragging his or her feet in spiritual matters? Sooner or later, you should be able to discern how spiritually mature the person is. Does he or she participate in a Bible study? Does he or she attend church when you're not there? Does he or she participate when a discussion turns to God? Is his or her spiritual interest authentic?

The following are some obstacles that can threaten any dating relationship:

Going out with someone else. Often on a first date, people exchange pertinent information. You tell the other person what your plans are in life, what your likes and dislikes are, and how "available" you are. If you are up front and say something like, "I'm dating someone else at this time, but we're not going steady or anything, and I thought it would be fun to get to know you," that says one thing. But if you don't disclose the other person, and the person you are trying to get to know finds out, that's dishonoring to the relationship and grounds for breaking it off.

The same goes for a more advanced relationship in which you both "know" that you are exclusively dating each other. If the other person starts seeing someone behind your back, that does not bode well for the future of the relationship. Cut it loose.

Pressuring you for sex. If that's all your dating partner

has on his or her mind, throw him (or her) back into the water. That's no catch.

Is not a go-getter. Do you notice that when your date is at your place, you're always serving him or her? If s/he's content to plop on a couch and watch TV all afternoon while you keep the snacks coming—and never offers to help out, not even with the dishes—that could be a signal of what is to come. Is s/he a conscientious student? Does s/he hustle at work? What's his/her work ethic like? Does s/he try to get by with the minimum, or does s/he try to beat expectations? Does s/he look for ways to grow and develop skills? Does s/he take initiative?

Comes from a seriously dysfunctional family. If you start dating Kelly Osbourne and she asks you to come over to "meet the parents"—Ozzy and Sharon—well, just remember that you don't marry just one person on your wedding day. You marry her family as well.

We're not suggesting that you should immediately break up with someone from a dysfunctional family—after all, most families have some level of dysfunction. But we are saying that if you see serious dysfunction—physical or constant verbal abuse, debilitating addictions—be on the alert. Just know that the person you are dating not only has had poor models but also is probably processing lots of issues in his or her own life. Remember too that Christ can make huge changes in a person's behavior and personality. Just know that your relationship will face some unique challenges.

AMY SAYS

If, after praying and exploring the questions and obstacles we've listed, you decide that you need to break up, how will you do it? Or if you are the person who is the recipient of the bad news, how will you handle it?

We've already touched on the difficulties I had when Jeff, my boyfriend throughout college, broke up with me. I could not handle the rejection. I jammed my foot into the door and tried to keep a toehold on the relationship. I plotted for ways to make Jeff come back to me. You know the rest of the story.

I couldn't bring myself to see that Jeff was not the right person for me, especially after he took the first step and suggested that we not see each other so that he could concentrate on his senior year of schooling. I clung to the hope that he would come to his senses and come running back to me.

I don't know what I was thinking at the time, but what happened to us was perfectly normal: When a relationship starts to fall apart, we have a tendency not to think clearly. We are almost sure to make mistakes, say the wrong thing, leave false impressions, or turn the whole thing into a huge misunderstanding.

There's a lesson at work here: The longer you two are together, the more difficult it is to break up, move on, stop seeing each other, say good-bye, stop going out, call it a day, part company, say *arrivederci*—whatever you want to call it.

Drawing on experience and the mentoring Michael and

I do with young people, we suggest that you be praying and asking God for direction when you feel the relationship is not what you want it to be. We are all inadequate when it comes to these matters of love, and we're as clumsy as a gorilla playing a violin.

Jeff and I made another mistake when we mutually agreed to "remain friends." That left the door open to continue calling each other after it was over. Every time Jeff phoned—which was around once a month—his voice dredged up all sorts of feelings inside me. I began imagining what it would be like to be officially back together. I turned those daydreams into a plot to win him back. Once he saw the error of his ways, he would apologize and open his arms to welcome me back into his life.

Here's what I've learned: When you make the break, follow it through. Don't take long walks wondering how you can turn the situation around. What's past is past. Leave it there.

Michael and I recommend that you *not* call the other person to check in or to "see how you're doing." It doesn't change anything, and in the long run, it's only going to stir up turmoil in you and your former dating partner. This doesn't mean that you look right through the person if you happen to run into each other between classes or at the mall (you can certainly stop for a neighborly hello), but don't go out of your way to maintain contact via the telephone, e-mail, or Instant Messaging. It's best to get on with life and see what the Lord has in store.

MICHAEL SAYS

When the moment of truth comes, know what you're going to say, and follow through on your commitment to break up. You could say something like:

"Lindsay, I've been doing some soul searching about this, but I've come to the conclusion that we should not go out together anymore. This is very painful for me to discuss, and I know it will be difficult for us to talk about, but I feel this would be the best for both of us."

If you're a young woman talking to a guy, expect the arguments to fly. (Trust me, I know.) He will have an answer for every objection you raise. Remain committed to your course of action. If he asks for reasons why, you may have to be circumspect, since the truth can also hurt. In other words, if he's a lazy bum, drinks and takes drugs, has bad breath, whatever—he's not going to respond well to your perspective of his flaws. Stay focused. Talk about the direction you want to take in life or how you want to move on or how you feel the relationship is not the one you see going the distance. Soften the blow by saying, "I'm sure God has someone else out there waiting for you."

We know that when the Lord is working on one side of the relationship, he's also working on the other. Nothing passes his in box without action.

When you're a guy breaking up with a young woman, be prepared for a flood of tears. You have just tapped a deep reservoir of feelings, and she will probably unleash a torrent of emotions over your head. *You never did like me.*

... You're so stupid.... I don't see why I ever went out with you. ... Nobody loves me.... I don't know what's going to happen to me....

Affirm her, but maintain your resolve to end the relationship. Again, that's the key here. Once you feel that this dating relationship is one you don't want to continue because you don't see this person as marriage material, it's best to cut it loose and make a clean break. From our counseling experiences, couples who break up, then get back together, then break up, and get back together are usually not the couples who make it to their fifth wedding anniversary, let alone their fiftieth.

When Amy decided it was time to break off her relationship with Jeff—and don't forget that they were engaged to be married at the time—she knew there was no getting back together. She says it wasn't fun explaining why she no longer wished to marry him, followed by returning the engagement ring to him. But she had to do it. The old saying "Better a busted engagement than a busted marriage" is still true today. So is "Better a busted dating relationship than a busted engagement."

Let me make an important point about all this breaking-up business that should help you keep some perspective. We have a tendency to believe that the sun won't rise in the east the morning following a breakup. Your world is shattered, and all you can see are the shards of your life lying on the ground. You wonder if you can pick up the pieces and get on with your life.

But you can. I have done it. Amy has done it. Most people have done it.

It's not easy. But if you trust that God is leading you, then you will also have the confidence that he will show you the next steps.

That about wraps it up. Let's conclude this book where we started, with a paraphrase of Scripture:

> Be strong with the Lord's mighty power. Don't date naked. Clothe yourself with all of the protection God has provided so that you will be able to stand firm against all strategies and tricks of the Devil. For when you date, you will face temptations and challenges that are beyond your ability to fight alone. You will need God's grace, love, wisdom, and power. You will need help from friends who are committed to your good. You will need a special wardrobe for the challenge.
>
> So get dressed. Put on all of the clothing God has provided so that you will stand firm. Stand your ground, putting on the robe of prayer, which will cover you, submitting yourself and your future to God's plan. Next put on the sturdy belt of accountability, which will hold you to your goals. For shoes, put on honor so that you will be able to walk confidently, giving full respect to the people you date. In every dating situation you will need a commitment to purity as your shield to stop the fiery arrows of temptation aimed at you by Satan.
>
> Pray at all times and on every occasion in the power of the Holy Spirit. Stay alert, and be persistent in your prayers.

So, keep the right clothes on. Don't date naked.

Dear Mike & Amy,

Do you believe that God has just one perfect person for each of us?

—Just Wondering

DEAR JUST WONDERING,

LET ME (MICHAEL) ANSWER THAT QUESTION IN TWO PARTS.

IS GOD INVOLVED IN OUR FINDING A SPOUSE? ABSOLUTELY. DOES HE KNOW THE PERSON WHO IS BEST FOR US? YES. THAT'S WHY IT'S SO IMPORTANT FOR US TO BE PRAYING. DO I BELIEVE THAT I WOULD HAVE HAD A GOOD MARRIAGE WITH MY HIGH SCHOOL SWEETHEART, STACY? I WOULD SAY YES. WE ENJOYED A HEALTHY RELATIONSHIP WHEN WE WERE TOGETHER. SHE'S A GOOD CHRISTIAN WOMAN, AND I'M A GOOD CHRISTIAN GUY. BUT GOD HAD A BETTER PLAN AND MOVED US APART. IF I HAD NOT ACCEPTED THAT GOD WAS IN THE BREAKUP, I WOULD NOT HAVE FOUND AMY.

HOWEVER, MAYBE YOUR QUESTION IS REALLY THIS: IS THERE ONLY ONE PERSON MEANT FOR YOU? IF THAT IS THE CASE, THEN I WOULD ANSWER A BIT DIFFERENTLY. DO I BELIEVE AMY IS THE ONLY ONE FOR ME? THE ANSWER IS YES—AND NO. YES, SHE IS THE PERSON GOD SELECTED FOR ME TO MARRY. BUT IF, GOD FORBID, AMY WERE TO DIE, WOULD THAT MEAN THAT I COULD NEVER FALL IN LOVE AGAIN WITH SOMEONE ELSE AND GET MARRIED? NO. AMY AND I DON'T BELIEVE THAT GOD HAS ONLY ONE PERSON MEANT FOR EACH OF US. IF SHE DIED, I BELIEVE I COULD LOVE ANOTHER PERSON, BECAUSE LOVE IS NOT AN EMOTION AND IT'S NOT A FEELING. LOVE IS A DECISION.

—Mike

Dear Mike & Amy,

Should you always break up in person?

—A Bit Scared to Break Up

Dear A Bit Scared,

We would say that it's best to break up in person, especially if you have had a long-term dating relationship. It shows respect for the other person as well as for your relationship.

That doesn't mean it's easy. You might want to prepare the other person a bit by saying something like this: "I've sensed a change in our relationship, and I thought it might be good for us to talk about it. Can we do that sometime soon?"

If you break out in a cold sweat just thinking about breaking up, then you could express your desire to break up in a letter. Some of us are personality types (like Stewards) that don't like confrontation and can't stand the pressure of verbalizing feelings.

Let the Golden Rule be your guide. Break up with the other person the way you would want the other person to break up with you. Okay, we understand—who would *want* someone to break up with them? But I think you get the point. Do a careful job. Pray. Be kind but honest. Leave the person's dignity intact. Honor him or her even in the way you break up.

Is a "Dear John" e-mail acceptable? While it's not preferred, it can be done, but only if your relationship has been short and you have normally communicated by e-mail. However, it's rather impersonal to use an IM session to tell someone you're breaking up.

—Mike & Amy

NOTES

Chapter 1: Let's Hear It for Dating

1. U.S. Bureau of the Census (1998), "Marital Status and Living Arrangement," (March 1997). See <http://www.census.gov/prod/3/98pubs/p20-506u.pdf>, as quoted in a footnote to Andrew R. Baker, "Cohabitation Fails As a Test for Marriage," *Homiletic & Pastoral Review* (May 2000); <http://www.catholic.net/rcc/Periodicals/HPR/May00/marriage.html>.
2. Larry Bumpass and Hsien-Hen Lu, "Trends in Cohabitation and Implication for Children's Family Context," unpublished manuscript (Madison, Wisc.: Center for Demography, University of Wisconsin, 1998), as quoted in a footnote to Andrew R. Baker, "Cohabitation Fails as a Test for Marriage," *Homiletic & Pastoral Review* (May 2000); <http://www.catholic.net/rcc/Periodicals/HPR/May00/marriage.html>.

Chapter 5: Sex and the City

1. Lorraine Ali and Julie Scelfo, "Choosing Virginity," *Newsweek* (December 9, 2002): 61.
2. The Koop quotation and the comment about the sores are found in Kevin Leman, *Adolescence Isn't Terminal,* (Wheaton, Ill.: Tyndale House, 2002), 191–92.
3. *OB/GYN News,* 28:15 (1993), quoted in "Condoms Ineffective against Human Papilloma Virus," *Sexual Health Update* (April 1994): 1.
4. Kenneth L. Connor, "Powell's Reckless Remarks Put Young Lives at

Risk," *The Family Research Council* (February 17, 2002). See also
<http://www.frc.org/get/ar02b2.cfm>.

5. Larry Bumpass and Hsien-Hen Lu, "Trends in Cohabitation and Implications for Children's Family Contexts in the U.S.," Center for Demography and Ecology, University of Wisconsin–Madison, NSFH
Working Paper No. 83 (June 1999): 16–17.

Chapter 6: Staying Safe While Dating

1. Merriam-Webster's Collegiate Dictionary, 10th ed., s.v. "date rape."

2. We are indebted to Dr. Gary and Barbara Rosberg for these steps,
which are explained more fully—especially as they relate to conflict in
marriage—in their book *Healing the Hurt in Your Marriage* (Wheaton,
Ill.: Tyndale House; and Colorado Springs, Colo.: Focus on the
Family, 2004).

ABOUT THE AUTHORS

Michael and Amy Smalley both earned master's degrees in clinical psychology from Wheaton College Graduate School. Michael, an author and speaker, is currently the president of Smalley Family Outreach, a nonprofit ministry dedicated to creating a global marriage revolution through training international pastors, missionaries, and lay leaders. Amy is also an author and speaker, offering topics on women's issues, and is involved in monthly marriage and couples counseling "intensives" through the Smalley Relationship Center.

For the past seven years Michael and Amy Smalley have spoken live to thousands of people. Their message is simple and applicable to anyone in any situation: Honor God and others before yourself. They teach with entertaining stories and illustrations to allow their audiences to enjoy the time and learn with laughter. The Smalleys have spoken to groups ranging from singles conferences to marriage seminars and parenting seminars. The topics they cover are as varied as the groups. They also lead an active youth group at Woodland Hills Community Church.

Michael and Amy have three children—Cole, Reagan, and David—and have been married for nearly a decade. They make their home in Branson, Missouri.

Contact information on next page

To find out more about the resources, conference schedules, and counseling services of the Smalley Relationship Center and Smalley Family Outreach, use these contacts:

The Smalley Relationship Center
1482 Lakeshore Drive
Branson, MO 65616
Phone: (800) 84-TODAY (848-6329)
FAX: (417) 336-3515
E-mail: family@smalleyonline.com
Web site: www.smalleyonline.com

Smalley Family Outreach
1482 Lakeshore Drive
Branson, MO 65616
Phone: (866) SFO-8442 (736-8442)
FAX: (417) 334-8250
E-mail: info@smalleyoutreach.org
Web site: www.smalleyoutreach.org

SMALLEY RELATIONSHIP CENTER (SRC)

Our mission is to create a marriage revival throughout the world by increasing marital satisfaction and reducing the divorce rate.

ENRICHMENT PRODUCTS

The SRC has more than 50 marriage, parenting, and relational books, videos, and audiotapes to enrich all of your most important relationships.

PROJECT SMALL GROUP

We are calling men and women to become "Marriage Champions" by taking the step of becoming marriage small-group leaders. Our Web site offers not only eight different series that you or your church can order but also support for leaders.

SMALLEY ON-LINE

Our Web site provides weekly e-newsletters, new articles on marriage and parenting, interviews with authors, and on-line enrichment through marriage and personality profiles. Preview or order our latest resources @ **www.smalleyonline.com**

COUNSELING SERVICES

Intensive Marriage Counseling

During the "intensive" you and your spouse will spend two days (Marriage Intensive) or four days (Couples Intensive) with our marriage specialists in Branson, Missouri. This concentrated time allows you to rapidly move down to the root of your problems in a way that traditional weekly therapy cannot duplicate.

Phone Counseling

Are you having trouble finding a Christian counselor in your area? Do you want to work with a pastoral counselor who knows how to apply the teachings of the Smalleys? Phone counseling might be the perfect fit.

SMALLEY FAMILY OUTREACH (SFO)

SFO is our international outreach ministry to educate and equip pastors, missionaries, and lay leaders on how to save marriages in their own countries! Find out more about how we are having an impact on marriages and families worldwide @ **www.smalleyoutreach.org**